ARTIFICIAL INTELLIGENCE

ARTIFICIAL INTELLIGENCE

THE SEARCH FOR THE PERFECT MACHINE

Lawrence Stevens

HAYDEN BOOK COMPANY
a division of Hayden Publishing Company, Inc.
Hasbrouck Heights, New Jersey

Acquisitions Editor: Prijono Hardjowirogo
Production Editor: Dennis Mendyk
Copy Editor: Christopher Jaworski
Cover Design: Jim Bernard
Cover Photo: Pete Turner/The Image Bank
Text Design: Sharyn Banks
Illustrations: John McAusland
Compositor: Vail-Ballou Press, Inc.
Printing and Binding: The Maple-Vail Book Manufacturing Group

Library of Congress Cataloging in Publication Data

Stevens, Lawrence
   Artificial intelligence, the search for the perfect machine.

   Bibliography
   1. Artificial intelligence. I. Title.
Q335.S84 1984   001.53'5   84-25195
ISBN 0-8104-6327-X

1	2	3	4	5	6	7	8	9	
85	86	87	88	89	90	91	92	93	YEAR

Preface

In this book, we provide the reader with an understanding of the many worlds of AI research. The majority of the book discusses the different AI projects, such as expert systems, natural-language programs, and robotics. We will also look at early attempts to solve simple problems. We will see the philosophical foundations of creating thinking machines and the physiology of machines that mimic human thinking behavior. The ideas of those who feel that AI is impossible on practical and philosophical grounds will be given a hearing along with the idea that applied AI will provide mankind with a brave, new world. We will also touch on some basic information on how AI is programmed.

As you will be able to tell by a glance at the table of contents, we have tried to present as complete an overview of the subject as can be accomplished in one volume. This necessarily means a good amount of selectivity in what is discussed. If you want to pursue any particular AI subject in more detail, you should find ample references in the bibliography.

Technical aspects of AI are included with the goal of providing the reader with a general understanding of how AI programs work. No attempt could be made to provide enough information to allow the reader to program AI. Such a project would require devoting at least one volume to each of the chapters. And there are many books already available that serve that purpose.

What has been lacking in the field of AI literature is a comprehensive, mostly nontechnical, book covering many different aspects of the field. The purpose of this book is to attempt such an overview.

Contents

ARTIFICIAL INTELLIGENCE

▪ ONE ▪

BACKGROUND

· 1 ·

Artificial Intelligence: An Overview

The goal of artificial intelligence (AI) researchers is to produce computers that act in a way that is analagous to intelligent behavior in humans. At first blush, it might seem that all computers act that way when solving, say, an algebraic equation or when counting the number of employee sick days over a year. But to act intelligently—to think—means more than to figure, more than to calculate, more than to match letters and numbers. To think means, among other things, to combine new information, previously known facts, rules of thumb, guesses, and even intuition to come up with an appropriate response to a problem.

If all this seems a bit unclear, it is because it is still vague what actually happens when people do think. We all know what "thinking" is, but to define the act so that it can be used as a test for determining if a computer has thinking ability or intelligence is a task not yet accomplished.

To simplify this problem, computer scientist Alan Turing has devised a test that eliminates the need to define intelligence in terms of what one does when one acts intelligently. The Turing Test can be stated simply: If a human can question a computer, receive answers (through an intermediary), and not be able to determine if he or she is communicating with a human or with a machine, then the machine can be said to have intelligence.

This test, while adequate for determining if a computer can think just as a human does, cannot fully determine if the computer is acting

3

intelligently in limited spheres of activity. This is important because modern AI researchers do not expect in the near future, or perhaps ever, to create a machine that can think and act intelligently in as many different spheres as a typical human is capable of. A more realistic expectation of a machine is one that might, for example, be able to "see" and perceive the world and make certain interpretations about its perceptions. Another machine might be able to understand ordinary English and to translate it into a programming language. A machine could possibly pass the Turing Test if it were questioned only on oil drilling technology, but it would fail totally if it were questioned on proper manners in restaurants.

While limiting the scope of what a single computer can do, this process allows artificial intelligence to be a real possibility rather than a dream. But it also clouds the issue as to what intelligence is and what it is not.

All computers, even unintelligent ones, compute better than humans, and humans think better than computers. Often, computers can use their ability to juggle large amounts of data quickly to perform tasks that, if performed by a human, would require intelligence.

For example, suppose you worked in a small office and were asked if a certain Jim Brown worked with you. Instantly, you know that no one named Jim Brown works there. How do you know? You may say that you quickly matched the name Jim Brown with every name at work and came up with zero—in other words, you proceeded as any computerized database management system would have proceeded.

But suppose you worked for a company with 100 employees, all of whom you know by name. When asked about Jim Brown, you know instantly that the name does not "ring a bell." Psychologists are uncertain how humans accomplish this, but it is probable that the speed with which answers are given indicates there is no matching of data. But we cannot be certain what *does* go on in your mind; so, to compare human intelligence with machine intelligence, it is necessary to compare only what we *do* know: behavior.

When we look at behavior and compare it to the operation of computers, we discover that even ordinary computers can search names faster than humans can go through whatever process they use to search names. We return then to the Turing Test: If a computer can act in a way that appears similar to the way a person would act in a similar situation, is that computer acting intelligently? On one level, the answer has to be yes. After all, you have no way of knowing what is going on in someone else's mind. All that anyone can perceive is action. You may try to explain what is happening in your own mind, but you could easily be wrong or lying. And, of course, a computer can be easily programmed to "explain" what goes on in its "mind." We may not believe the computer, but because thinking is a subjective experience, it is impossible for anyone but the thinker to know for sure what is happening. So we must use human behavior, not subjective statements about what a human does when he or she thinks, as a guide for determining intelligent behavior in machines. By using this as a guide, the ordinary computer in the example above is able to act at least as intelligently as a human.

But few AI researchers consider an ordinary database management system to be an example of intelligent behavior. The reason is that this particular activity stacks the deck unfairly in favor of the computer. As we pointed out, things like matching and doing arithmetic computations are what the computer does best. A better example is the playing of a game of chess. Again, we will use our criterion: Do a computer and a human act similarly? And to make the test fair, let's compare the computer to a chess master rather than just to a typical human. After all, any computer can be programmed to make random—even legal, random—moves and lose a game just as a poor chess player might.

Okay, you are a chess master. How do you act? In general, you move in such a manner that you usually get a favorable board position. If a computer played chess in a way similar to that of matching names on a list, it would examine each legal move available along with every possible consequence of each move. But to do this for a normal chess move would take present computers from now until the sun burns out. Clearly, here is an example of where the computer cannot use its brute strength to masquerade as a sentient being.

To program a computer to play chess, the researcher must try to determine how the chess master thinks. This is done not to test whether the master is acting intelligently, but rather to get some clue as to how to program a computer to perform in a similar manner. At each board position, you apply certain rules that allow you to make a decision on a move after examining, say, only five or ten possibilities. For example, you try to control the center squares. Or you do not bother to examine certain classes of moves. Because a chess board is laid out much like a graph, the researcher realizes that translating board positions into symbolic language is not difficult. Also, it is not too difficult to program the rules of thumb that are used by a master in playing the game. (When programmed into a computer, the rules of thumb are called *heuristics*.) For these reasons, chess-playing computers, and those that solve "brainteaser"-type puzzles, were the first examples of artificially intelligent machines.

Other problems are more difficult. Another area of AI research is that of natural language. The goal of natural-language researchers is to create a machine that can understand human language, just as an intelligent human can. This task, as we shall see later, is a lot more difficult than simply having the computer match entered words with an internal dictionary. The computer must be able to understand inferences and references, for example. Even a sentence as simple as "This is the boy who gave me the book" presents the problem of programming the ability to understand that "who" equals "boy" in that sentence. Other sentences require an understanding of the story that surrounds them. For example, "We had a sale today" might mean that we sold something today or that we lowered our prices today. The only way to know which is meant is to understand the context in which the sentence is quoted. Young children quickly pick up the ability to understand language; computers have a long way to go before they can accomplish this satisfactorily.

Another example of an AI project is that of image understanding. Computers have long been able to interface with cameras that enter information about the world. But to have computers understand what they "see" is a problem that has plagued AI researchers. In an extremely controlled environment in which the computer "looks" for a limited number of objects, much progress has been made. But put a robot equipped with a vision system in a cluttered construction site, and it will probably trip over the first unexpected object in its path. Problems are enormous. For example, the computer has to make out the significant edges of objects. It must understand that a door is one object, despite the fact that there may be six panels and a number of cracks that form edges but do not enclose an object. And the computer must be able to understand when smallness represents distance and when it represents diminutiveness. In this area, computers are not yet functioning at the level of a three-year-old child.

WHAT AI CAN DO FOR US

A glance at Part Two of this book provides an overview of the large agenda of AI researchers. This agenda encompasses much of human mental activity. Although it is unlikely that a computer containing all these abilities will be developed in the foreseeable future, computers that can do some of these things—often interfacing with other computers that accomplish other tasks—are being developed and improved. The result is a substantial increase in the usefulness of computers.

In general, the practical purpose of creating intelligent computers is to allow them to perform tasks that are either too difficult or too distasteful for humans to be able to do or to want to do. These machines will include robots that do factory work, mining, and even household domestic chores; "in-house experts" that will advise humans; and machines that automatically control energy plants, factories, and homes. To the extent that the AI agenda is successful, all human life on this planet will be transformed. Research into cures for disease and into engineering problems will be speeded up and will be made more economical by expert machines that can solve problems themselves as well as provide information that will assist humans in that function. Physicians who are finding it difficult to keep up with new information will be able to access machines that will have expert medical knowledge and will be able to diagnose disease and even prescribe treatment. Structures will be built by robots, and robots will direct activities. Mines will be worked by robots that need no oxygen, food, rest, or recreation (and humans need not risk their health and lives).

The availability of natural resources and human productivity will increase tenfold or more. There will be more food, more products, and improved health. Assuming man overcomes the political and economic problems of distributing this new wealth fairly, there will be no poverty or even drudgery.

Although all this might be an overly optimistic assessment of what AI can do for humans, there are many scenarios along the road to that image of the future that, though perhaps not as grand, are certainly most welcome. We already see how robotics has resulted in higher productivity in many industries. Further improvements in this field are certain to hasten that trend. There are already medical-advice machines that assist physicians in diagnosing disease. Natural-language systems assist non-computer-oriented people in gaining access to data bases. No matter how far AI technology is able to go, improvement in our quality of life is certain to accompany any success.

▪ 2 ▪

A Brief History of AI

The early history of the quest for artificial intelligence takes two main routes, the first based in fantasy or sometimes in magic, the second based in science. The former was concerned with automata, robots, and mechanical humans. The latter was concerned with describing human reasoning in terms of scientific or, to be more precise, mathematical theories.

AI IN MYTH

The literary and oral traditions of automata are rich. Back in the Middle Ages, for example, Pope Sylvester II claimed to have a fortune-telling robot that would respond with "yes" or "no" when asked questions. Also in the Middle Ages, a group of Arab astrologers claimed to have created a thinking machine called the Zairja, which could hold forth on philosophical subjects.

Ramon Lull, a 13th-century missionary who had attempted to convert Muslims, transported the idea of the Zairja to Europe. Lull's machine, called the Ars Magna, was said to be able to reason on Christian topics. The Ars Magna was made up of metal disks that could be spun. After each disk came to a stop, a number was displayed. This number was matched against a table that contained the various categories of thought. And by matching the numbers on the various disks in various ways, a sort of philosophical answer to any question was offered.

Reasoning machines in the Middle Ages tended to be defenders of the then-current religious climate. The Church, after all, was the only center of learning. But later, as people became more secularized and began to explore the true sciences, different kinds of mechanical humans and reasoning machines were invented. In the 14th century, clockmakers produced gigantic clocks with figures that moved and sometimes spoke. These clockmakers, of course, did not claim to have invented thinking machines. But the public, seeing such large moving figures, often thought of them as mechanical humans, and stories of these figures coming alive began to abound.

Paracelsus (1493–1541), who had held a chair of Physics and Surgery at Basel, had, he claimed, discovered a recipe for the production of a mechanical human:

1. Take some human sperm.
2. Enclose it in a hermetically sealed jar.
3. Bury it in horse manure for 40 days.
4. When it is dug up, it will resemble a human except that it will be somewhat transparent.
5. It should be fed with human blood until it is 40 weeks old. After that, it will be able to survive on its own.

Paracelsus then gave specific instructions as to its education. After such education, this reasoning creation would be a perfect human.

In 1580, Rabbi Judah ben Loew claimed to have created an artificial human who could walk among the Gentiles of Prague to find out if one of the recurrent pograms was at hand. The rabbi created his figure out of clay from the banks of the Moldau. After incantations and the inscription of the Holy Name on the creature's head, the human came to life. The rabbi named his creation Joseph Golem. The creature not only spied on the Gentiles but also did chores around the synagogue and the rabbi's house.

During the next two centuries, the increase in mechanical technology caused mechanical humans of the clockmaker's type to increase in number and sophistication. They were found in all the great cities of Europe—moving arms, legs, heads, and even talking and answering questions.

In the 19th century, mechanical and artificial humans, which were much more sophisticated than those that adorned the castles and cities, began to appear in literature. In 1815, E.T.A. Hoffmann wrote *The Sandman*, which includes Olympia, a mechanical woman. In 1870, Delibes wrote the ballet *Coppelia*, in which a mechanical doll comes alive. Of course, one of the most famous artificial humans in 19th-century literature was *Frankenstein*.

AI IN SCIENCE

All this does not illustrate humankind's ability to create machines that think, but rather its wish to do so. In the early 19th century, however, work began in earnest on thinking machines. The first problem, and a continuing problem, was to represent knowledge in a way that could be manipulated by machines. And, of course, in these early years, manipulation meant mechanical (and not digital) manipulation.

Development of Digital Machines

George Boole, a 19th-century mathematician, took a step in the digital direction with his Boolean algebra. This was a binary system that could represent not only numerical functions but also elementary logical functions. Variables were represented in terms of A and B, true and false, or 1 and 0.

In part using Boolean algebra, Charles Babbage, in the middle of the 19th century, was the first to design a digital computer; he called it an analytic engine. The analytic engine was to compute by counting wheels that turned one way or the other, depending on input. Punched cards were used to gain access to the machine.

Probably the most important advance provided by Babbage is that his computer design was truly digital. Many previous and later designs were for analog computers, which do not truly compute (they measure). These machines might measure the distance a cog traveled or the length of the exposed part of a ruler. A digital computer, on the other hand, determines if very sharp differences exist. For example, a digital computer might determine if a circuit is on or off. The logic parts of digital computers are like light switches that are either on or off. They count how many are on and how many are off, and do the calculation. The logic of analog computers is measurement, temperature measurement, for example. Analog computers measure the temperature of this room, then measure the temperature of that room, then measure the rooms together (but do not add them together) to get the combined temperature. The problem with analog machines is that they are cumbersome to program. It is difficult, and in many cases impossible, to represent many forms of knowledge and to do calculations through measurement.

The problem with digital machines, however, is that you need the technology to represent these distinct on and off states. And because this technology was lacking in the 19th century, Babbage's machine never was built.

The most important technology for representing on and off states is, of course, the electric switch. And soon after this was developed, the first digital computer was built (in 1944 by H.H. Aiken). The machine used telephone relay switches—3,000 of them. It was cumbersome and very slow. But it was a start. And the world was ready for the next generation of digital computers, the kind that work with vacuum tubes.

The introduction of digital computers represents the first advance of artificial intelligence. The biggest step represented by digital machines over analog machines is that they can be programmed to do (at least in theory) any type of logical calculation. Any mathematical symbols can be represented, any instructions can be entered, and any output can be requested. Each analog machine was built for one purpose—to measure a specific thing or to add or subtract only. The difference between analog and digital machines is the difference between an adding machine and a calculator. But in a larger sense, it is the difference between an automatic welding machine and a robot that can do many things besides weld. You cannot say that an automatic welding machine is intelligent. It is simply a set of gears and cogs that move so many inches in one direction, so many feet in another direction, and so forth. But a robot that can be programmed to weld today, fasten bolts tomorrow, and carry boxes the next day comes close to our idea of an intelligent worker.

As digital technology was being developed during the 1940s, the dream of developing thinking machines was being shared by many researchers. This dream, though, also disturbed some people at that time. Consider the words of Sir Geoffrey Jefferson:

"Not until a computer can write a sonnet or compose a concerto because of thoughts and emotions felt, and not by the chance fall of symbols, could we agree that a machine equals brain—that is not only write it but know what it has written. No mechanism could feel (and not merely artificial signals, an easy contrivance) pleasure at its successes, grief when its valves fuse, be warmed by flattery, be miserable at its mistakes, be charmed by sex, be angry or depressed when it cannot get what it wants."[1]

The Turing Machine

Turing answered this challenge by saying that there is no way that any of us can know, using Jefferson's definition, that anyone thinks. If a machine, through "artificial signal," states that it feels pleasure, how can anyone know whether it does? How is the machine's statement different from a human's? We assume that when other humans say they are happy, they have approximately the same feeling that we do when we say we are happy, but how can that point be proved? Turing said it cannot be. As a result, he developed the Turing Test described in Chapter 1.

Although Turing was not the first to build a digital computer, he is often called its father because of his successes both in theory and in practice. In 1937, he wrote a paper called "On Computable Numbers," in which he proposed that certain mathematical problems could not be solved through any "definite process." To define "definite process," he described an arithmetic machine. This machine, which became known as the Turing Machine, was built (in theory only) to test whether certain classes of problems could be solved digitally. Anything the machine could not do could not be solved through a definite process.

Ironically, although the machine was introduced in the paper for a negative reason (that is, to show what the machine could not do), what it can do is very interesting. It functions by having a long strip of tape passed through it. The tape is divided into sections. Each section either is blank or includes a punched symbol that stands for a number. The tape passes through the machine one section at a time and moves forward or backward, depending on instructions received from the machine. And, even though there are many operations the machine cannot do (as the paper points out), it can perform any operation that can be expressed in Boolean algebra, that is, any operation that can be expressed in terms of 1s and 0s.

AI Research and War

A version of the Turing Machine was built for the British government in the 1940s. Many historians credit it with the winning of World War II.

The story of this first use of the Turing Machine is interesting in light of the fact that many present-day AI projects are funded by defense organizations. Near the beginning of the war with Germany, England captured an Enigma Machine, a coding/decoding device used by the Germans. The machine was contained in a portable box. In many ways, it resembled a typewriter, except that there were a number of wheels between the keys and the print heads. To code a message, the sender simply moved the wheels to a specific number and typed as usual. The typed message came out in code. To decode a message, the receiver set up an Enigma Machine in the same way the sender did and typed the received message. The British had no problem reproducing and fully understanding the workings of the Enigma Machine they captured. The problem was in discovering the correct setting of the wheels. Occasionally, the correct setting could be found through luck. But a day or so later, the settings would change, and the process had to begin over again.

The machine that could determine the settings almost on a daily basis was invented by Turing and others working with him. Based on the Turing Machine, the machine became known as the Bombe. When a message was received, the first six letters (representing the settings of the Enigma) were fed into the Bombe. The machine then spun and tested all possible combinations of letters until one that lead to a message that made sense was reached.

Other Avenues of Research

These early thinking machines, while powerful for their day, did not even come close to passing the Turing Test. They were able to perform very specific problems in a logical order (preset by the thinking humans who programmed them).

For machines to think, rules had to be found that could describe thinking. Instructions had to be programmed into a computer to allow it to perform such thinking activities as game playing and theory solving.

Many early AI researchers decided to examine the rules governing the thinking involved in game playing, which did not require large data bases (not technically feasible at the time). And yet, there was complete agreement that game playing required intelligence.

In 1955, the first chess-playing computer was built. It played a slow, poor game. But it did make only legal moves. It was a beginning. By 1957, a program was built for the IBM 704 to play plausible, amateur chess.

Another line of artificial intelligence was being followed by Anthony Oettinger. In 1952, he created a machine that could learn in an almost Pavlovian manner. It was able to alter responses to certain questions based on positive and negative reinforcements.

After his successes in that area, Oettinger worked on a mechanical dictionary that could automatically translate English into Russian and vice versa. He hoped that the mechanical dictionary could not only match words but could also eventually associate words with objects—the beginning of natural-language processing.

"Abstract" AI Research

Oettinger had only very limited success with his dictionary. He also lost track of his original goal of discovering a general rule or set of rules governing intelligent behavior. Probably the main reason for his failure was that his projects were important enough in themselves to cause Oettinger to develop means of solving problems that had nothing to do with intelligence.

To get at this more general set of rules, Alan Newell and Herbert Simon analyzed the way students solved problems. One thing they discovered was that students often took shortcuts. These shortcuts did not always lead to correct solutions of a problem; occasionally they arrived at a dead end. But statistically, over the course of an hour or so, these shortcuts cut down the time required to solve a set of problems. And in some cases in which time was limited or the problem was so immense, shortcuts were the only feasible way to solve a problem.

These shortcuts were dubbed *heuristics.* They are problem-solving methods that may not lead to a solution but that offer a shortened path toward the solution. The opposite of heuristic problem solving is algorithmic problem solving. An *algorithm* is guaranteed to lead to a correct solution. Most AI programs developed by Newell and Simon, as well as present-day programs, are combinations of algorithms and heuristics. Algorithms are used when feasible; heuristics are used when shortcuts are needed, as in a game of chess.

The discovery of heuristics was an important event in the history of AI. Newell and Simon wrote an article called "Empirical Exploration with the Logic Theory Machine; A Case Study in Heuristics." It describes programming the computer to use these heuristic shortcuts to solve theorems. But more than simply solving problems, the machine showed how problems were solved. This would be a great help in further AI research. The paper states:

"The research reported here is aimed at understanding the complex processes (heuristics) that are effective in problem solving. Hence we are not interested in methods that guarantee solutions, but which require large amounts of computation. Rather we wish to understand how a mathematician for example, is able to prove a theorem even though he doesn't know when he starts how, or even if, he is going to succeed."[2]

Newell and Simon felt that their Theorem Prover was not general enough. It was able to provide heuristic information that would be used in theorem solving, but it could not tell how heuristics would be used in other areas. So in 1957, Newell and Simon built their General Problem Solver (GPS).

While GPS is discussed in detail in Chapter 14, the method the GPS uses can be stated simply as follows:

1. Determine the difference between the present situation and the goal.
2. Find some action that reduces this difference and perform that action.
3. Determine if the final goal has been reached. If so, then end. If not, go back to step 1.

Newell and Simon called this type of heuristics *means-end*. For a problem to be solved through means-end heuristics, it must have the following characteristics:

1. The difference between the present situation and the goal can be detected and quantified.

2. Operators or actions can be classified by how they affect the difference between the present situation and the goal. Some operators lengthen that distance, some do nothing, and others shorten that distance. And of those that shorten the distance, some have a great effect, some a small effect, and so on.

3. Some differences are difficult to affect using any operator. It is therefore necessary at times to substitute new differences for the old ones. The adjusted distance might be exactly the same as the original distance, but at least the operators can work. If you have to get to work and your car won't start, you might walk to the bus stop, which is a mile in the "wrong" direction. But there you have the opportunity to affect the difference between your present location and work.

The GPS was able to solve very simple problems. But in problems that are so large that the possible actions or operators became so great that the search was impractical, it did not work. Discussing the GPS, AI researcher Marvin Minsky pointed out that "in more complex problems where the search space grows larger, each trial becomes more expensive in time and effort. One can no longer afford a policy of simply leaving one attempt to go on to another."[3]

The *neural-net* approach to AI was based on physiological considerations. Brain cells were not very specialized, and most cells could perform many different functions. For example, if a set of brain cells is killed as a result of an accident or disease, another set of brain cells could take over the function formerly performed by the now-dead ones. Brain cells organize themselves into behavior patterns—for example, those governing speech, hand movement, and so forth—through learning, experience, perceptions, and so forth. Researchers tried to ape this brain ability by creating systems that could organize themselves in similar ways. These were called *self-organizing systems.*

One such system was called Perception, which was developed at Cornell by a group of researchers headed by Frank Rosenblatt. On the outside of this system was a group of photocells that were meant to correspond to the human retina. These photocells were sensitive to light. Inside the machine, cells collecting light input transmitted from the photocells passed it on to response units. Perception could classify information that it received. For example, if its input were a series of lights blinking on and off in a certain order, it could ape this series in its output. It could then remember the pattern and repeat it on command.

AI Back in the Real World

Perception was an interesting machine in that it was a bold attempt to imitate the brain. But as a useful invention or even as a prototype that might breed useful inventions, it fell short. Its main problem was that, although it could repeat the signals it received and could even classify them, it had no means of representing knowledge symbolically. Using such a system is akin to trying to describe a story by acting out all the parts rather than by using words.

Difficulties with the Perception project led many AI researchers to turn away from the hope that an intelligent machine could be built by copying the physical structure of the brain. The brain was, and still is, mostly incomprehensible to humans. We do not understand how it works. But we can study the mind, at least in some ways, by studying how humans solve problems.

Language Translators

Another important project was the building of language-translation machines in the 1950s. We already spoke of the work of Oettinger and his mechanical dictionary. Oettinger's program simply matched one word with another word or words. It did not understand words in context, as a translation machine would. As Oettinger said, "The main problem of selecting an appropriate target correspondent for the source word on the basis of context remains unsolved."[4]

In the late 1950s, a $20-million program on machine translation was launched, but to no avail. And even today, there is little talk of reviving this project, although some of the barriers to contextual understanding have been broken.

In the 1960s, Daniel Bobrow developed one of the first programs that attempted to understand some English, STUDENT. The purpose of the program was to solve algebraic problems using plain English input. Although not very effective by today's natural-language standards, STUDENT was able to break down sentences into such functions as multiplication or addition and unknowns into Xs and Ys. It worked well with restricted sentences, but it became stuck often and had to query the user for information.

In the late 1960s, Thomas Evans produced a program that could solve analogy-type problems. It reportedly could solve the "this is to this as that is to that"-type problem as well as a tenth grader could.

These currents of research began to come together in the 1970s. During that decade and in the early part of the 1980s, most of the programs and knowledge described in Part Two of this book were developed. For many applications, from problem solving to natural-language processing to image-understanding systems, the 1970s was the time when AI became a practical science. And now, in the 1980s, further progress has allowed AI programs to leave the universities and earn their way into the real world.

▪ TWO ▪

PRACTICAL PROGRAMS

· 3 ·

Natural-Language and Voice-Recognition Systems

For many computer users, communicating with their machines is a frustrating experience. Just when a user seems to be moving along just fine with a database management system or spreadsheet program, the computer displays an enigmatic error message. Sometimes the message is a terse "?". At other times, it is as confusingly expansive as "WRONG DATA RETURN TO PRIOR ENTRY AND REENTER."

Error messages like these are becoming less common in the present age of the "friendly" computer. Many programs are now more forgiving in their acceptance of entries and more helpful in explaining user errors. But user-friendliness has its limits. And the point can still be made that the more powerful a program is, the more difficult it is to set up and use.

This problem has caused many people to avoid the computer. Although few businesses lack computers today, many still keep them in the back room; the machines are guarded by a group of cognoscenti who know how to speak computing languages.

To speak to a computer, a person must learn a specific subset of English. Current user-friendly programs try to confine this subset to familiar English words, but only specific words can be used and they must be entered in a specific manner.

AI researchers working on natural language (NL) are attempting to program the computer to understand not only this English subset (often called computerese) but all English words and sentences used in human-to-human communication. As one researcher-cum-salesman said,

"In order to sell to the guy on top, we have to develop a machine that will allow him to type 'How's business?' and get an appropriate response."

Cognitive Systems Inc. of New Haven, Connecticut, is one company providing natural-language front-end systems. A front-end system is an interface between a user and a data base. It allows the user to gain access to the data base by typing plain English sentences.

Cognitive Systems's programs understand sentences in context, resolve pronoun references, make inferences, sort ambiguities, unscramble ungrammatical sentences, and allow use of references.

Here are some examples of interactions with Cognitive Systems's programs:

1. *Implications:* If a user types "Who has owed us money for more than two months?" or "What customers have unpaid bills for more than sixty days?" or almost any other sentence that means the same thing, the computer will display appropriate accounts receivable information.

2. *Ambiguities:* Notice how the word *sale* has a different meaning in each of these sentences—"What is the average markup on sale of stereo equipment?"; "What is the average markdown during a sale of stereo equipment?" A natural-language program is able to sort the ambiguities resulting from ambiguous uses of a word. In the first sentence, it understands that "sale" means a business transaction; in the second sentence, it understands that "sale" is an activity in which prices are reduced.

3. *Ungrammatical sentences:* Most business memos are written in short, often cryptic, and ungrammatical sentences. This "news headline" communication is easily understandable by all people in the same business, and it provides a quick method of communicating. Such sentences as "Flights NY to Chicago next Thursday" and "ITT averaged net gain week of July 1" can be understood by natural-language programs that are prepared to respond to profession-specific code words and slang.

4. *References:* During a session at a computer, the user will often need to refer to information acquired or entered in a previous interaction. For example, the user may type "Show me oil wells drilled prior to 1970 in Bibb County, Georgia. The scale should be 1" to 2000'." Once the information from the data bank is received, the user would be able to type "How about since 1970?" without retyping all the information about location and scale. Natural-language programs are capable of understanding references to past interactions.

SYNTAX AND SEMANTICS

Natural-language systems interpret sentences in two ways, syntactically and semantically. Syntax is the study of the form of a sentence and is concerned with parts of speech, the object and the predicate of a sentence, and other formal aspects. Semantics is the study of the meaning of the sentence and includes the meaning of the individual words as well as the meaning of the sentence as a whole.

For a sentence to be understood, a program must be equipped to work with both the syntax and semantics of language. Syntax is important in that it provides the first clue as to the meaning of a sentence. Consider the famous sentence from Lewis Carroll's poem "Jabberwocky":

'Twas brillig and slithy toves
Did gyre and gimble in the wabe.

We do not know the meaning of most of the words, but we can interpret the syntax of the sentence. Ignoring the possibility of unconventional or incorrect usage, we can say that "toves" and "wabe" are nouns, "brillig" and "slithy" are adjectives, and "gyre" and "gimble" are verbs.

Using this information, we can make tentative guesses as to the category to which each word belongs. We can guess, for example, that "brillig" is an adjective that describes a scene or, more likely, the weather. It might mean "hot," "warm," or "cloudy." "Brillig" could of course also be a noun such as "Sunday" or "summer." But even in that case it would refer to a state of being, "summer" meaning "hot," for example, or "Sunday" suggesting "a slow, lazy day." "Toves" is capable of doing at least two things ("gyre" and "gimble"). We might guess that it is not a hole or a rock.

Obviously, we do not have to look far to see that these guesses can be wrong. (A loose rock could vibrate and shake in the wind!) Syntactic understanding provides certain clues to meaning, but it cannot provide a definitive decoding of a sentence. Nevertheless, it is the first step toward decoding. We will begin here by looking briefly at the general processes used by NL programs in deciphering the syntax of a sentence.

Subject and Predicate

There are hundreds of rules of grammar. Among the most basic of these are rules governing the structure and position of the subject and predicate. This is a good place for a program to begin working on a sentence because all complete sentences have both a subject and a predicate. In other words:

SENTENCE = SUBJECT + PREDICATE
and
SUBJECT = ARTICLE, ADJECTIVE(S), NOUN,
PREPOSITIONAL PHRASE(S).

In the sentence, "The blue car on the left struck the tree," "the blue car on the left" is the subject.

The one necessary part of the subject (the noun or pronoun) is called the simple subject. The noun and the (optional) words that surround it are called the complete subject. The rules governing the complete subject are as follows: There can be only one article for each noun, but there can be many adjectives or prepositional phrases for each noun; the order of elements—article, adjective(s), noun(s), prepositional phrase(s)—must be adhered to if the sentence is to be grammatically correct.

The prepositional phrase can also be broken down into parts. It must contain (in this order) a preposition and a noun or a noun phrase. In the sentence "The car on the right side of the road struck a tree," "on the right side of the road" is the prepositional phrase. "On" is the preposition, and "the right side of the road" is a phrase with one article, one adjective, one noun, and one prepositional phrase.

Here is a simple illustration of how a program breaks down and syntactically decodes a sentence.

1. The first routine determines if the group of words is in fact a sentence. This requires two subroutines. The complete subject subroutine checks for the required parts and structure of a subject. If a subject is found, the object (or verb) subroutine checks for a verb.

2. If the group of words is a sentence, the complete subject subroutine takes over. This subroutine hands control to the article subroutine, which contains a list of articles. If it finds an article, it registers that fact; if not, it registers "no article" and returns control to the complete subject subroutine.

3. The complete subject subroutine then hands control to the adjective subroutine, which searches for adjectives and registers any it finds or "no adjective."

4. If the adjective subroutine registers positive for an adjective, the complete subject subroutine hands control back to the adjective subroutine to search for another adjective. This continues until the adjective subroutine comes up with a "no adjective" message.

This process is continued until all parts of the complete subject are classified.

While each element of the sentence is identified as a certain part of speech, it is also identified in other ways. A noun, for example, can be identified as referring to an animal, plant, object, person, and so forth. Sex and occupation can also often be determined. An adjective can be classified as a color, a size, a shape, or within another category. These classifications can be accomplished primarily by matching the words in the sentence against those in a dictionary.

Once a sentence is broken down into parts of speech, and as many words as possible are categorized, some assumptions can often be made as to the function of each word in the sentence. This process begins to bridge the gap between syntactic and semantic understanding.

Here are some possible types of nouns.

1. *Agent:* initiator of the main action in a sentence.
2. *Instrument:* object used by the agent to initiate the main action.
3. *Medium:* material through which the agent initiates the main action.
4. *Source:* place where the main action begins.
5. *Destination:* place where the main action ends.
6. *Route:* path the instrument takes in going from the source to the destination.
7. *Conveyance:* conveyer of the instrument from the source to the destination.

There are many ways to determine the functional category into which a noun might fall. One clue is provided by the meaning of the verb in a sentence. For example, a verb that describes animal motion (such as running, strolling, and sauntering) suggests that the order of nouns in a sentence will be agent, possibly route, and then instrument. A verb that describes human-controlled motion (such as driving, riding, or sailing) suggests the possible presence of a conveyance. The preposition "with" suggests the presence of a co-agent, and so on.

All other parts of speech can be categorized in a way similar to that used for nouns. For example, verbs can be categorized as move-instrument, transfer-possession, and move-self. For each of these categories, there are clues—similar to those used with nouns—that allow a program to classify words by function.

Of syntactic and semantic understanding, the latter presents by far the thornier difficulties. This is because humans often speak in ways that do not conform to simple rules. Implications and ambiguities abound; they are used because they make communication more efficient and because a human with particular knowledge can easily infer an idea suggested by other humans who share that knowledge. The phrase taught to thousands of students as an example of a dangling modifier—"While sitting on benches, coffee and donuts were served"— is unambiguous to most people, but it is still grammatically incorrect. It is difficult, however, to program a computer to understand that the coffee and donuts are not sitting on benches.

Solving Ambiguities

Ambiguities can arise when the speaker assumes—usually correctly—that the listener knows more than is intended in a sentence. For example, if someone asks for "spaghetti with tomato sauce and wine," how will the various foods be combined—spaghetti with tomato sauce and wine in the same dish? Obviously, the wine is meant to be served separately. On the other hand, if someone asks for cereal with bananas and milk, it is probable that the speaker wants to combine these foods in the same bowl. The reason a computer has difficulty with these sentences is that the key to understanding them is having knowledge about eating habits; having knowledge about words is not enough.

Many NL researchers are working on the problem of making inferences, of picking up implications. Eugene Charniak of the Institute of Semantic and Cognitive Studies (Switzerland) has developed five topics that must be addressed by AI researchers in order to develop systems that can understand ambiguous implications:

1. *Semantic representation:* What specific concepts do humans use in recording their impressions of the world?

2. *Inference triggering:* Under what circumstances do people make inferences? When should a computer be on the lookout for an inference-dependent meaning?

3. *Organization:* When an implication is made, how does the computer know where to look for the object of the implication? In the sentences about the food, what tells the computer to search its data base of information about eating habits instead of its data base of information about, say, wine making?

4. *Inference mechanism:* Once the facts related to the implication are found, how can a program make use of them?

5. *Content:* What world knowledge is required for the computer to understand language?

Providing a program with inference mechanisms is most easily done in question-and-answer sessions that are prevalent in, say, expert systems. (See Chapter 4.) The two most common times when a user would make an implication are when the computer asks a question that requires an inference and when enough information is given to make an inference.

Knowing when to begin looking for implications, though, is only the first step. The next step is either to make sense of the implication (to disambiguate) and to store the information in the data base with the object of the implication defined, or to store the information with the implication remaining ambiguous.

There are advantages and disadvantages to both alternatives. If the implication is to be inferred before it is stored in the data base, a lot of computer time may be spent making trivial inferences that may never be needed. If, on the other hand, the implication remains ambiguous, it may be necessary to store with it all the knowledge that might be needed later to understand the implication. This creates a problem with space.

To develop rules as to when an implication should be made unambiguous, researchers have turned to psychological studies to determine how humans deal with ambiguity.

A well-known and often-repeated experiment consists of providing people with reading passages. Later, the people are asked if they remember specific parts of the passages. However, these parts are not explicit in the reading material; they are normally inferred from it. In almost all cases, the subjects "remember" the inferred facts. Although the test does not result in conclusive information as to when the subjects make their inferences—at reading time or at questioning time—the fact that their subjective experience is of remembering facts leads many psychologists to believe that inferences are made at the time of reading.

The results of this study point to one of the problems with AI research in general. Often, because human-like intelligence is the goal, AI program developers look at human behavior as the means of obtaining this goal. Their hope is that a machine that acts exactly as a human acts would also have human-like intelligence. But the fact is that the human thinking mechanism is probably quite different from a digital computer in many ways. And even if it can be proved that humans make inferences when ideas are first implied, it does not necessarily follow that using this knowledge will provide the most expeditious way to program a machine.

The computer may also make inferences based on whether they are problem-occasioned or non-problem-occasioned. A problem-occasioned inference is one in which the information cannot be comfortably assimilated by a human without first understanding it. This is because the structure of the sentence itself is ambiguous. For example:

"John bought a hat. When he got home, his wife said, 'You already have one, take it back.' "

Interpreted without knowledge about stores and the fact that only recently purchased items may be returned, the preceding sentence may seem to imply that John's wife wants him to return the hat that he had already owned. To understand that the word "it" refers to the new hat, not the old one, we need to know that stores do not usually take back old hats. This is a problem-occasioned inference, because leaving the fact in the sentence ambiguous would probably mean assimilating incorrect information. It is extremely likely that humans make this inference when they hear the sentence.

If the computer were to store this information without making the inference, it would be necessary to store information about stores and about how to return items (or at least pointers to those subjects) along with the implication. As it is likely that the inference would need to be straightened out at some point in the process, making the inference ahead of time would seem to be an economical approach. Furthermore, other parts of the story might bear on the inference. Suppose John had just bought his old hat two days ago. In this case, his wife could very well have been referring to the old hat. The computer would have to determine if there are any such parts of the story that relate to this inference, and it would store them as well. It is very cumbersome, if not impossible, by present technology to store all the information that could possibly have an effect on the meaning of the sentence along with the ambiguous problem-occasioned inference. So, understanding before processing is the only practical method.

A non-problem-occasioned inference is one in which there is no structural ambiguity in the story as a result of the inference. Understanding implications of the story, however, gives the reader more information that he or she may need later. For example:

"The car skidded off Highway 56 and hit a tree."

You can infer that the tree is somewhere near Highway 56. You can also infer that a human driver is in the car. These implications do not make the sentence ambiguous. Understanding it may be useful, depending on what you are asked to do with the information. If a computer, for example, had to summarize a news story that includes that sentence, understanding the implications may perhaps become necessary. But it is not likely. Therefore, storing the information with the ambiguous inference is economical. Even if we take humans as a model for a program that can understand the sentence, it is unlikely that they would reflect on the information before assimilating it. And if they were asked about the setntence later, they would most likely not have false recollections about explicit statements placing the accident near Highway 56.

Another time when an inference must be made at reading time is when a lot of information has to be stored in the computer to allow it to make the inference later. For example, Charniak provides the following statement:

"When Flint was very small, his two elder brothers, although they sometimes stared at him, paid him little attention. Occasionally when he was grooming with his mother, Faben gently patted the infant."[5]

The problem here is to determine who "he" is, Faben or Flint. The reader, as it turns out, requires a lot of information to solve this. Actually, the reader must read a large part of the entire story to understand the implication. The characters are actually chimpanzees. Flint, a baby chimp, does not groom, so the "he" has to refer to Faben. If a program were to leave this ambiguous, it would have to be ready to access a good part of the story that contains information about the identity of the characters as well as about chimpanzee behavior. This would require a lot of pointers to be programmed along with the implication. It is much less cumbersome in this case to analyze the implication before internally representing it.

Another type of inference that should be analyzed before internalization involves a speaker who is suspected of exaggerating or lying. If a salesperson says, "My store offers the lowest price in town," it is normal to suspect (even to assume) that he or she is exaggerating. It would be a mistake for programs to take all statements at face value. In fact, if you consider all hyperbole, white lies, exaggerations, and outright deceptions used during the course of any day, you may find that five percent or more of all statements are not complete truths. This is not a judgment about morality, but rather a statement about language conventions.

Although outright deceptions are not a function of language and have little relevance to a discussion of inference, certainly exaggeration or hyperbole should be inferred in many situations. A program must have a way of determining why someone may lie, and, when it detects that someone is lying, it must be on the lookout for untruths. There are many such examples of untruths. For example:

1. Salespeople tend to exaggerate the relative value of their products.
2. Employees tend to compliment their bosses falsely.
3. Parents tend to deny many negative aspects of life when talking to their young children.

Obviously, the fact that someone is lying is easier to store than all the information about an individual that would allow a computer to later piece together the information to infer an untruth.

The problem of when to make an inference—at reading time or at questioning time—then becomes one of finding a middle road between storing too much information and wasting computer time by making unnecessary inferences. The computer must therefore be able to distinguish between inferences that it will likely or will not likely have to use.

Identifying Key Ideas

So far, we have discussed the ways that a program can decide what to include in its internal representation of a statement. This internal representation must be able to work with other data. That other data must be called up at certain times and must be suppressed at others. Charniak's system calls for a sort of "key idea" pointer in the data base.

For example, in the sentence, "If it rains while we are outside, we will get wet," the key idea is "rain." The program must be able to call up its data on rain. But it must suppress other data that might be called up by that sentence. For example, "outside" is not a key idea. The program can determine that rain is the key idea because the action of getting wet occurs almost only when it rains, and rain almost always causes getting wet. On the other hand, going outside does not always result in getting wet. And going outside makes many other things possible as well.

The computer having this knowledge will call it up whenever it reaches the word "rain." But it will also be able to use its world knowledge to call it up when rain is implied, as in "As Jack was playing golf one afternoon, the sky grew very dark. He decided he had better get inside fast." To associate these sentences with rain—and, therefore, to call up the information about getting wet in rain—the program would have to be supplied with the following statement: "When the sky gets dark during the afternoon, rain is likely."

Further world knowledge must be used to suppress calling up pieces of information that may falsely seem relevant. For example, when confronted with "Jack has a ball," the program would likely call up its knowledge about Jack (or about men) and about balls. But let's look at a few possible instances in which calling up that knowledge would not be appropriate.

1. "Jill was going to buy Jack a ball, but she changed her mind when Mary said, 'Jack has a ball.' " In this sentence, we are not really concerned about the ball as an object or about Jack as a person. Rather, we

are concerned about the fact that when someone has X, he or she probably will not want to buy X. The operative words are "buy" and "has."

2. "John wanted to play baseball. Suddenly he saw Jack walking by and said to himself, 'Good news! Jack has a ball.' " In these sentences, the idea is that if a person has X, he or she might want to use X. This would not be stored under "ball" or under "Jack" in a data base because it is general information that could be used for many objects.

3. "John's kite was stuck in a tree. He looked around for something to use to get it down. Then he saw Jack and said, 'Jack has a ball.' " In these sentences, we are finally using the word "ball" in an exclusive sense. There are only a few objects that can be used for the purpose at hand, and a ball is one of them. Information about this use of a ball could very well be stored under "ball." Of course, the information would also be stored under "projectiles" and other related subjects.

Charniak identifies a "bookkeeping" section as another part of an inference program. This updates the story as it progresses from point to point. For example, in "John traded his ball for Bill's bat," the story changes. Who now has the ball? Who now has the bat? The program must keep track of these events, but it must not lose sight of who previously had each item because that information might also be important.

The program must also provide some mechanism for pointing backward from various uses of an object to the object itself. In "John got his umbrella because it looked like rain," the question is "Why did John get an umbrella?" It would easily be answered: "To keep the rain off his head" by following the pointer from umbrella to its use. Also consider this sentence: "John saw that everyone but he was carrying an umbrella, and he began to worry." To understand why he was worrying, the program must be able to start with the use of the umbrella and point back to the object.

Information is stored in the program in data structures that Charniak calls *frames*. Each frame is in the form of a statement that describes a stereotypical situation. For example, "SHOPPER obtain use of basket" would be a frame for a supermarket situation. The word SHOPPER is capitalized because it is a variable. If the program came across "John went to the supermarket and took a basket from the parking lot," the program would gain access to its supermarket frames and plug in JOHN for SHOPPER.

Another frame is "SHOPPER obtains PURCHASE-ITEMS." This would be called into play when the program sees a sentence such as "John bought eggs, milk, and butter."

Also in the frame would be a probable sequence of events:

1. SHOPPER obtains basket.
2. SHOPPER obtains PURCHASE-ITEMS
3. SHOPPER pays for PURCHASE-ITEMS
4. SHOPPER carries PURCHASE-ITEMS TO VEHICLE.

Programming this sequence allows the system to identify certain actions, as in "John paid Harry ten dollars before they entered the store." If it were not for the sequence that lists "pays for PURCHASE-ITEMS" after "obtains PURCHASE-ITEMS," there would be a problem in programming the computer to understand that John was not paying for his purchases at that time.

Sometimes, though, actions will be out of normal sequence. In this case, the program could deal with it by flagging the aberration. For example, because "John carried his groceries to his car and then went and got a basket" is out of sequence, it might be of interest later. So, it is worth the extra computation required to store this out-of-sequence information as an unusual event.

Sequencing is also helpful in making more difficult inferences. Consider the following sentences:

"John pushed his cart over to the milk shelf and picked up a quart of milk. He then paused to consider what to buy next. Finally, he walked over to the cheese counter and put one pound of cheddar in his cart."

Q: Did John put the milk in his cart?
A: Probably.

Most people would agree that "probably" is the correct answer (as opposed to "I do not know"—which in some cases is the most appropriate response). The computer would be able to respond similarly because of the following sequence:

1. SHOPPER puts PURCHASE-ITEM (n) in cart.
2. SHOPPER puts PURCHASE-ITEM (n + 1) in cart.

The second item, the cheese, would not be put in the cart until the first item, the milk, was placed in the cart. This is of course not always the case, but the fact that most people would answer the above question as "probably" shows that such an assumption is worth making.

But a program must also be able to deal with situations that are not the norm. Flexibility must be built into the frames to account for many different situations. For example, not all shoppers choose to use a shopping cart. And that is not abnormal and should not trigger the flagging of an aberrational situation. There are two possible solutions.

One is to create two separate frames, one for shopping with a cart and one for shopping without a cart. Although this method solves some problems, it creates a gigantic data base with much redundancy.

Another solution is an if/then type of statement. For example:

1. SHOPPER decides whether to use a basket. If yes, then basket = T (for true).
2. If basket = T then SHOPPER obtains a basket.
3. SHOPPER obtains PURCHASE-ITEMS.
4. If basket = T then SHOPPER puts PURCHASE-ITEMS in the basket.
5. If basket = T then SHOPPER uses it to convey PURCHASE-ITEMS.

And so on.

These frames can be very useful in programming many different situations. For example, suppose a practical joker removed all the items from John's basket and put them on the floor when John was not looking. It would be impossible to include in the supermarket frames information about practical jokers and other unexpected situations. And because the question "Why did John pick the items up from the floor and put them in his basket?" would be an easy one for humans to solve, the computer cannot respond to that question with "I do not know, it is an aberration." But, using the supermarket frames along with the sequence, the program would have a way of fathoming this unusual situation. It would not be able to explain why the joker put the items on the floor (unless, of course, it had frames about jokes), but it could use sentence 5 above to figure why John put the items back into his cart (to convey them).

Obviously, the example above provides only a small number of frames necessary to define a supermarket situation. But the idea of using frames does provide an economical way to program a large amount of knowledge into a natural-language program.

SPECIFIC NATURAL-LANGUAGE PROGRAMS

SAM

SAM (Script Applier Mechanism) is a program (actually a series of programs) that was built to understand stories. It has been able to summarize newspaper articles.

Knowledge is given to SAM in the form of scripts. A script is a scenario of what generally happens in a given situation. For example, an auto accident script contains information about what happens when autos collide: what happens to the vehicles, what happens to the occupants of the vehicles, what the police might do, and so forth.

When the program senses an accident in its reading of the news, it looks for clues that will answer certain questions. Were the police called? Was anyone killed? Was anyone hurt? What was the extent of property damage? And so forth.

Another script is an oil-spill script. In this, the computer looks to see if oil escaped, and if so, how much. What animals were threatened by the spill? What plants were threatened? And so on.

All scripts in SAM are ranked according to their importance in bringing about the main action of the story. Steering the car, for example, is a subscript in the process of driving, and driving is a subscript in the process of taking a trip. And even trips may be major trips or side trips (subscripts of main trips).

Whenever SAM encounters an event, it first determines which script should be used. It does this by searching for words that provide clues to the proper script. The words "auto" and "crash" used in the same story would result in the activation of the auto accident script. Once SAM finds the correct script, it hunts for words that show that certain actions in the script have occurred. For example, the word "killed" would activate the part of the script involving personal injury, and the word "police" would activate the script involving legal activity.

SAM makes three main inferences in analyzing a story. They are causal-chain completion, role instantiation, and role merging.

Causal-chain completion allows SAM to infer the intervening events in a story that gives only the first and last events. In "John walked to the subway station. He went to the express platform," there is much missing between the two events. After he went into the subway station, he probably went to the turnstile, he probably put a token in the turnstile, he probably pushed the turnstile, and so on. SAM is given scripts for various events, such as walking into the subway, that allow it to fill in the blanks in causal chains.

Role instantiation is information about what people or things tend to do in various situations. For example, a script can explain what people do on subways. If, for example, "John walked to the subway" is followed by "John was home within the hour," role instantiation will allow SAM to guess that John rode the subway home.

Role merging allows the computer to assume that, because people who walk into subways tend to go to a platform, the "he" in "John walked to the subway. He got on the express platform" probably refers to John. This is because John is expected to do what the "he" in the sentence has done (i.e., "John" and "he" are merged).

Let's look at a small part of input to and response from SAM.

INPUT: A car swerved off Route 69. The vehicle struck a tree. The passenger, a New Jersey man, was killed. David Hall, 27, was pronounced dead at the scene by Dr. Dana Blanchard, Medical Examiner. Frank Miller, 32, of 593 Faxen Road, New Haven, Connecticut, the driver, was taken to Milford Hospital by Flanagan Ambulance. He was treated and released. No charges were filed. Patrolman Robert Ontorio investigated the accident.

SAM'S SUMMARY: An automobile hit a tree near Highway 69 four days ago. David Hall, age 27, residence in New Jersey, the passenger, died. Frank Miller, age 32, residence at 593 Faxen Road in New Haven, Connecticut, the driver, was slightly injured. The police department did not file charges.

SAM is also able to answer questions about a story. For example:

Q: Was anyone hurt?
A: Yes, Frank Miller was slightly injured.

Notice in the story that there is no mention that Frank Miller was injured. The program is able to make the connection between "hospital" and "being injured." This is accomplished using the script that explains what happens in hospitals.

SAM uses role merging to connect the vehicle that hit the tree with the car that swerved off the road. It uses the same technique to connect David Hall with New Jersey.

And finally, there is nothing in the original story that states the accident happened near Highway 69, as SAM asserted. SAM is able to use the time and place setting of the story to understand where things probably happened based on the time of the occurrence. As cars swerve only for a short period of time, the swerve must have ended and the accident must have occurred near the point that the swerve began.

SAM works well with stereotypical events that conform generally to the scripts programmed into it. In the real world, though, events are often non-stereotypical. To tackle this problem, a program has been developed that can reason about motivation and intention.

PAM

PAM was developed to understand the motivation behind characters' actions in a story as a way of understanding the story itself. Consider these two sentences:

"John wanted to go to the movies. He called his friend and asked if he could borrow his sports car."

So far there doesn't seem to be anything here that would confuse SAM, assuming it was provided with appropriate scripts. For example, the script for "go" would include information about driving a car. But let's change the story a bit:

"John wanted to impress his date. He called his friend to see if he could borrow his sports car."

It would be almost impossible for a programmer to include scripts for all possible uses of cars or other objects. Cars are normally used for transportation; white T-shirts are meant to be worn. That cars can be used as a way of impressing a date and T-shirts can be used in a pinch as surrender flags will usually confuse a program that must rely on programmed scripts.

It therefore becomes necessary to provide the computer with an understanding of motivation and how goals are affected by various actions.

PAM understands four goal interactions:

1. *Goal subsumption:* PAM knows that sometimes many occurrences of a given action can be expected. "John liked to exercise before work. He bought a set of barbells." Here PAM is given to understand that when someone wishes to perform an act regularly, that person will act in a specific way. Buying something—e.g., barbells—is sometimes the prerequisite for repeated action.

2. *Goal competition:* "Bill wanted to listen to quiet music. But Bill's son put on rock and roll anyway. Bill broke his son's record in pieces." PAM knows that when two goals are in conflict, one must win and one must lose. The loser might react in an angry manner.

3. *Goal ambivalence:* This is similar to goal competition, except that the conflict resides in one person. "John had a date with Mary, but his friends wanted him to play softball with them. Mary wouldn't speak to John after that."

4. *Goal concord:* PAM knows that the goals of two or more individuals may sometimes be the same. "The driver waited in the car as the gunman walked into the bank. Five minutes later, the gunman, ducking bullets, ran to the car. When he got in, the driver sped off." To understand why the driver sped off, it is necessary to understand that the goal of each man was the same. Here is an example of PAM in action.

INPUT: John wanted money. He got a gun and walked into a liquor store. He told the owner he wanted some money. The owner gave John the money and John left.

Q: Why did John get the gun?
A: Because he wanted to rob the liquor store.
Q: Why did John threaten the shopkeeper?
A: Because John needed to get some money.
Q: Why did the shopkeeper give John the money?
A: Because the shopkeeper did not want to get hurt.
Q: Why did John leave?
A: Because John didn't want to get caught.

Notice that the first three questions and answers show the computer's understanding of why someone would buy a gun (goal subsumption). There is nothing in the story that states that John threatened the shopkeeper or that the shopkeeper was afraid of getting hurt. That was assumed from the fact that John bought a gun.

TALE-SPIN

Another program that uses goals as a method of understanding events is called TALE-SPIN. This program writes stories by generating behaviors based on goals that come out of previous behaviors. For example, "John wants to visit Mary" triggers the transportation goal, the communication goal, and so forth. Each goal thus triggered would in turn trigger another goal until the entire story is created.

TALE-SPIN begins by querying the user as to setting, characters, and some initial action. The program generates the rest of the story itself.

Each of these programs and others like them provide clues to the methods for full-scale natural-language systems. Each program in itself solves only part of the problem. Present-day working natural-language systems isolate the aspects of natural language that are required for each application. Few systems at this time need complete natural language (although no one denies that it would be desirable). The first goal, already reached, has been to create systems that function in a larger field of language than the conventional computer is accustomed to. The next goal is to constantly expand that field, just as children constantly expand their command of language.

VOICE-RECOGNITION SYSTEMS

It is probably safe to say that the most difficult task on the artificial intelligence agenda is the building of a system that can understand human speech. Rudimentary systems can recognize a very limited vocabulary spoken by a very limited number of people. These systems are, however, difficult to use. For example, each word must be spoken emphatically and must be surrounded by pauses. These systems are also prone to error. Unfortunately, systems that can understand everyday, fluent speech are many years in the future—if they are to be at all. Right now, we can discuss only the problems associated with building such systems and some ideas on how such programs would work.

Speech recognition is, in part, a subsystem of natural language. And therefore, even if the problems of recognizing speech were solved, the ability to understand speech would be limited by the state of natural-language technology. As mentioned earlier in this chapter, the ability to understand human language in a general way is still not possible.

Assuming the hurdle of natural-language understanding is overcome, the next problem to be solved concerns storing the patterns from which the program will find the internal representations of utterances. The problem is similar to that of pattern matching in image-understanding systems, which are discussed in Chapter 5. When a speech-recognition system receives a sound, it must find a similar sound or pattern in its data base. The nature of this data base is of primary concern.

The most direct method of building such a data base would seem to be to store an initial spoken vocabulary and then to have the computer build on that vocabulary as it comes across new words. But this task is a lot larger than simply storing the approximately 30,000 words in the average person's spoken vocabulary. The problem with the spoken word is that each different pitch, each different inflection, each different emphasis, no matter how slight, would result in the computer's "seeing" a new word each time. The computer would have to store every pattern of every word spoken by each user. And an individual's speech pattern is almost as unique as a fingerprint. There would be a constant need to store new words. Obviously, the size of this data base, along with the tremendous task of categorizing the stored information, makes this storage impossible.

But even if such a system could be built, a further problem exists. Research has shown that often there is not enough information in the audible signal that represents each word to signify what the word is. Words spoken in a sentence are often truncated, slurred, strung together—so that by themselves they bear little resemblance to the correct pronunciation of the words. In normal speech, a sentence cannot really be said to be made up of words; rather, it is made up of bits and pieces of words that are generally understood in terms of the sentence as a whole. Put another way, humans tend to understand complete sentences at a time, rather than individual words. So, a program must have an inventory of words as well as an inventory of sentences. Because the number of sentences in a language is much greater than the number of words, the problem of storage and retrieval is greatly compounded. One researcher estimated that there are 10^{30} sentences in normal spoken language. Even to input these sentences verbally would take about 1,000 man-years.

One possible solution is to ignore the words and the sentences initially and to break down the utterances into sub-word divisions. These divisions are called *events* or *distinctive features.* They are physical occurrences in the speech apparatus. Examples are the rate and amplitude of periodic excitation of the speech tract, the amplitude of aspiration, the amplitude and frequency of hiss noises, and so forth. Work has been done on developing systems that can sense these events from the uttered sounds. And it has been shown that these events are more standard in a language than in the spoken words and sentences of that language.

Once the computer receives and identifies sounds, it must match them up with corresponding patterns in its data base. It must use contextual clues to fill in gaps, as humans do when they miss a word. (Humans usually do not hear every word in a sentence; they rely heavily on contextual clues.) The computer must also abstract the most important parts of a sentence—once it gets to the sentence level—in a manner similar to finding the key concept in a natural-language program. It must be able to learn from its users and determine when querying users is appropriate and necessary.

Some AI researchers look at voice recognition more as an aesthetic goal than as a practical necessity. A computer's being able to understand human speech would be impressive. But there are viable alternatives to speech input; they may not be as convenient, but they would be as effective. For example, non-typing users can communicate with computers through "mouses," "touch screens," or sound input devices (e.g., touch-tone phones). Voice recognition must be compared with other AI projects, which seem destined both to have a broader effect on the human condition and to be easier to implement.

One argument in favor of developing spoken-language systems is that if a machine is to fully mimic human intelligence, it must be able to work with spoken language; second, machines may have to be used by everyone—even those unfamiliar with or those who do not want to use keyboards or "mousing devices"; third, voice recognition is another step toward computerizing drudgery (such as taking dictation, typing, or even programming) now performed by humans.

But no matter how important the development of voice-recognition systems is, one thing is clear: This technology involves so many divergent aspects of AI research as well as of hardware technology that its realization will come only after the full development of many other AI systems.

· 4 ·

Expert Systems

Expert systems are machines that think and reason as an expert would in a particular domain. For example, a medical-diagnosis expert system would request as input the patient's symptoms, lifestyle, test results, and other relevant facts; using these as pointers, it would search its data base for information that might lead to the identification of the illness. A circuit-troubleshooter expert system diagnoses problems in faulty circuits. A legal expert system advises users on points of law, and a geneticist expert system categorizes genes.

In a real sense, the creation of expert systems might be both the test of the possibility of machine intelligence and its most complete application. Ultimately, all AI systems may be connected in some way to expert systems. An image-understanding system that flies in a satellite to snoop on enemy ground forces would not only be able to relay data about those troops but would also offer suggestions as to the strategic and tactical significance of a troop buildup or reduction in a particular area. Natural-language systems that summarize newswire transmissions would also be able to include information on the implications of a piece of news. And robots that assimilate information about their environment would be able to use that information in scheduling production and in repairing broken machinery.

The development of expert systems—which has become a major part of AI research—is, in one way, an admission that a machine that can match humans in thinking ability might be beyond the possibility of present technology. Early AI researchers hoped to develop general thinking machines that could function as an average human in any situation. These attempts, such as the GPS described in Chapters 2 and 14, led to machines that performed poorly in many different domains. Gradually, the trend shifted toward the development of specialized programs. The theory behind this change is that it may be impossible to program the complete knowledge of even a 10-year-old child, but it is possible to program the specialized knowledge of an expert in a strictly defined domain.

Not only does this new trend represent developing a more realistic agenda, but it also begins to allow AI to move from sheltered (and often financially strapped) academies into better funded and more practical research areas. Suddenly, computer companies like IBM are becoming interested in AI. And small start-ups are jumping on the bandwagon. AI is an idea that can sell, and that is a sign that it is both useful to humans and that humankind is ready to accept it.

WHAT IS AN EXPERT SYSTEM?

The common digital computer, the ancestor of expert systems, allows us to compute large amounts of numbers quickly. It has been around for about 40 years and has become ever more sophisticated. Computer-aided drafting, for example, in its more sophisticated form, can be used to test for the break-point of each finite element of a design just by drawing the design on the screen. And there are legal programs that help an attorney find a case when key words that represent the type of cases are entered.

The reason these programs are not considered expert systems is that the way they approach a problem is predetermined by the programmer. They will match key words, do arithmetic computations, and use prespecified formulas. They do not, for example, choose to use a particular formula based on a rule of thumb; they do not come up with a new formula or idea when all else has failed.

A true expert system functions much differently. What it does with the information it receives is determined by the nature of the problem. It may shuffle and reshuffle the information until a solution is reached. A true expert system not only performs the traditional computer function of handling large amounts of data, but it also manipulates that data so that its output is a meaningful answer to a less than fully specified question. It can question the user for additional information, it can offer partial solutions when appropriate, it can make suggestions as to the general areas in which the complete solution may lie, and it can explain its reasoning process so as to act as a tutor and also to allow the user to evaluate the results. In other words, it can act much as a human adviser acts.

The machine is therefore the equivalent of a human expert seated in an extensive library containing many different books. The computer depends partly on its inhuman ability to sift through thousands of facts quickly. But it adds to that the definitely human ability to find short-cuts, to make and check hypotheses, and to test the relative validity of various solutions. This combination provides expertise in a true and useful form.

Problems in Expert System Development

As with all AI systems, the problem in development of an expert system revolves around the ability to represent the knowledge and skill of an expert in symbolic, computable language. Knowledge and skill are, of course, two separate fields, and each presents different prob-lems. Of the two, the easier to represent is knowledge—that is, facts. Storing knowledge is nothing new to computer scientists. Conven-tional data bases are, after all, nothing but collections of facts and pointers that allow organized access to those facts. To get these facts on record and to classify them so that they can be located when necessary, com-puter scientists must work closely with a team of experts in a given field.

Building "skill" into expert systems, however, presents more prob-lems. Skill consists of a list of heuristics, the rules of thumb, that pro-vide the "how to" in problem solving. These rules free the computer from searching its entire data base for an answer to a problem—a task as impractical for a machine as randomly searching every book in a li-brary would be for a scientist.

And finally, an expert system must contain the thousands of for-mulas and methods of reasoning that experts use in solving their prob-lems. Programming formulas taken from general textbooks is relatively easy, but sometimes the task with an expert system is to program the workings of an expert's mind. And, if so, we hit the problem that has plagued AI researchers from the start: If we do not know exactly how a mind works, how can we simulate it?

Discovering how a mind works in an attempt to build an expert system often falls upon the shoulders of knowledge engineers. These engineers spend days trying to get experts to explain how they solve a problem. Usually, it is at first difficult for experts to explain just how their minds work. One session of questions and answers may produce one set of routines, but when programmed, the routines may not pro-duce the desired results. Either the experts had not pinpointed their thinking methods correctly or the routines might work on only one small subset of problems. Perhaps the knowledge engineers failed to get the experts to generalize their methods sufficiently. Usually, the sessions go on for weeks; procedures and routines are refined each time and errors and misunderstandings are eliminated until at last there may be an approximation of the experts' method of thinking.

To date, these procedures have yielded mixed results. In areas in which knowledge can be easily categorized, as in medical diagnosis, systems can successfully search data bases and retrieve meaningful data. But in areas such as medical research, in which success depends more on a combination of facts than on searching through facts, results have been less than spectacular. It seems the step from standard database operation to expert system is in fact a number of small steps. Each system tends to be a little better than its predecessor in its need for fewer pointers and fewer instructions and in its improved ability to query a human.

SPECIFIC EXPERT SYSTEM PROJECTS

The rest of this chapter outlines some of the current expert system projects in the AI community. Many of these were reported in the Symposium on AI Technology Transfer at the "National Conference on Artificial Intelligence" conducted in Washington, D.C., in August 1983.

DART

DART (Diagnostic Assistant Reference Tool) is an expert system that diagnoses equipment failure. First, the user provides the system with the symptoms of failure. The system in turn suggests tests to be performed and accepts as input the results of the tests. It then attempts to pinpoint the faults that could be responsible for the problem. The project team, which began work in late 1980, is supported by IBM and is currently working on solving problems in computer hardware. Their system differs from many other expert systems in that it contains no information in its permanent data base about why equipment fails. It works by comparing information about the structure (i.e., the hardware) and the intended behavior of that structure. By noting differences between intended behavior and actual behavior (i.e., the symptoms), it pinpoints the difficulties. The advantage of this method is seen when a new machine is put into production, which normally requires adding information about the machine into the data base. (The expense of using the system would be high.) With DART, however, the user needs only provide information that is generated automatically during the computer-aided drafting of the hardware.

Currently, the DART team is at work on adapting the program to other types of equipment, including analog circuits and non-electric devices.

GUIDON2

GUIDON2 is a tutoring expert for medical students. It uses a medical consultative system called NEOMYCIN as a basis for its tutoring activity. NEOMYCIN is used because it is not only able to diagnose disease but it also outputs a diagnostic strategy. This output includes information on which areas to focus on, which questions to ask the patient, and which tests to perform. Although the program does not use natural language per se, it produces output in good, structured English.

With GUIDON2, the student receives information about symptoms and is expected to prepare a strategy for diagnosing the disease. The program summarizes the student's response, evaluates it, and provides alternative procedures.

KBVLSI

KBVLSI is a computer-aided design (CAD) machine for developing integrated circuits. But whereas most CAD systems simply provide the means for drawing a design on a screen, KBVLSI acts as an expert assistant to the designer. For example, the system will not let the user make certain improper connections. It can also define the behavior of any drawn circuit. Once a circuit is drawn, it can be tested from a number of different standpoints while it is on the screen. Also, when an overview of a large system is drawn, many subsystem parts are generated automatically.

MOLGEN

MOLGEN is a combined effort of AI researchers and biologists attempting to build expert systems that function in the world of molecular biology. One recent project in this area was the development of the SPEX system, which is a design system for cloning experiments. The system helps to design the experiment, to diagnose failed experiments, and to suggest corrective actions. The MOLGEN project team is working on a program that will allow the computer to closely mimic the way scientists work. This program will include theory formulation and testing, as well as theory restructuring based on information gained from experiments.

RX

The RX project team has developed a means of gaining access to medical information in a large data base. The system includes a knowledge base of medicine, statistics, epidemiological studies, and methods of discovering information. The knowledge base is used with a medical data base to automatically find relationships between input information and information contained in the data base. As of this writing, only a prototype system has been developed. It has been attached to the data base of the American Rheumatism Association and is successfully being used to find information without entering "keywords," as in standard database access methods.

IA

The goal of the IA (Intelligent Agent) project is to provide intelligent handling of data files in a large multi-user computer system. It will act as an operating system in functions such as rerouting electronic mail and scheduling user time. Commands to this operating system will be in high-level language, which may eventually switch to natural language; the project, however, is focusing more on what is called multiple-modality languages, which allow users to gain information through tables, charts, and diagrams, as well as through words. The system can retain user commands indefinitely and can act on those commands at appropriate times. It can also handle errors resulting from breakdowns on part of a system, from disk-space limitations, and so on.

MRS

The MRS (Metalevel Representation System) project team has developed an expert system that helps users to build other expert systems. It has domain-independent problem-solving strategies that can be used in a variety of expert-system situations. It has various search techniques, interface controllers, a truth maintenance system (for discovering logical truths), and a vocabulary of concepts. It also has the unique ability to reason about itself and to write routines for its own activities. The system has been used to develop many different kinds of expert systems, from a tax consultant to a simulator for digital hardware.

· 5 ·

Image-Understanding Systems

Designing programs that understand visual images—that "see" in the human sense—is necessary if AI researchers are to develop autonomous systems. Probably the most well-known image-understanding (IU) system is in the field of robotics. Providing robots with the ability to understand visual scenes is a prerequisite to developing a machine that can function without very specific programming. A blind man or woman can count on the versatility and adaptability of the human species to obtain nonvisual environmental input through touching, smelling, striking with a cane, or simply asking questions. To program this versatility into bulky and unwieldy robots would be more difficult than programming image understanding. Furthermore, IU systems would solve other robotic programming problems—trajectory problems (e.g., swinging an arm in the most economical way), locomotion problems, and so on. The automatic tooling process would not have to be programmed as exactly if the tooling mchine could "see" the part it was welding or the screw it was turning. Also, the difficulties in lining up parts would be much fewer with a sighted robot than with a blind one.

IU APPLICATIONS

Besides solving these problems, IU machines (both attached to robots and not) can perform many tasks (sorting parts into various bins, for example) that blind ones cannot. At present, the robot environment has to be structured by humans. This structuring includes setting up the various bins and feeders that will deliver parts to the robot. A fully automated factory would have the machines doing this structuring.

Another important task for an IU system is automatic inspection. As parts roll down the assembly line, they pass the camera of an IU system that triggers trap doors to discard defective material. This not only makes the inspection process less expensive, but it also tends to improve the quality of parts. A system like this could also be set up at the receiving area for inspection of parts received from other factories.

IU systems can also be used in medical diagnosis. Here a system could inspect X-rays, specimens, blood samples, and so forth for pathology analysis.

Sometimes maintaining an IU system remote from the area that it views can solve problems in information gathering. For example, in mapmaking, an IU system can be installed on a plane that passes over the area that is to be mapped. Hills, valleys, streams, rivers, and other landscape features are recognized and automatically drawn.

Another application is in traffic control. A camera attached to an IU system can be installed high above a busy traffic area. Using changeable message signs, the IU system can route traffic to ensure the most efficient flow based on up-to-the-minute information. Such a system could even tie into a voice synthesizer that would issue a continuous report of current traffic patterns to car radios. IU systems might eventually replace many air traffic controllers and boat dock traffic supervisors as well.

Oil and other resources can often be detected by studying surface features. An IU system equipped with geological information could assist in the search for natural resources in remote or hostile areas.

Similar uses could also be found in military applications. IU systems are already making rudimentary judgments about military installations and troop movements. IU systems could also be installed on missiles: A sighted missile would certainly prove even more effective than heat-seeking ones. Also, IU systems could allow artillery to track and fire at specific targets. And automatic navigation could be made possible using an IU system attached to the controls of an airplane or ship.

IU systems could be used along with conventional computer systems to make the computers more "user friendly." For example, users may only have to point to certain documents or objects to have the computer enter information. Or the computer may be able to accept handwritten or typed notes as input.

Akin to this function, reading computers could aid the blind by reading to them. Another system might describe a scene to assist the blind in getting around.

HOW IU SYSTEMS WORK

IU systems receive input from vision systems (most often TV cameras). Once the input is received, the first step is to understand the basic shapes (sometimes called *primitives*) that make up the scene. This is accomplished by using a series of patterns that are stored in the memory of the system. A pattern is simply a rule or rules that state which objects should fall into which categories. This allows the system to view a room, for example, not as a jumble of lines drawn helter-skelter, but rather as squares, or as rectangles and squares, or better still, as doors, windows, and tables.

Extracting and Quantifying Visual Characteristics

Recognizing objects is often accomplished by classifying them. The following figure shows a number of images that can be classified as "the letter X":

Although each X is a little different, establishing a rule or pattern to show what should fall into the X category would not be difficult. The rule would state certain facts about lines intersecting in a certain matter, and so on. The next figure shows a different group of objects—they are all different, but they can all be classified by one concept, "chairness." The chair pattern might include information about the number of legs, about the fact that there is an upright, a seat, and so on. Obviously, making a pattern for a chair is a lot more difficult than formulating one for the letter X because there are many more kinds of chairs than there are Xs.

A pattern-recognition program can perform a number of functions, among which are the following:

1. *Classification:* This is the basic function of most systems. When the program views one of the many types of Xs or one of the many types of chairs, a classification system places the item in the correct cat-

egory. It does this by matching the image with the pattern rules in its memory.

2. *Finding* or *matching:* This process is the opposite of classification. Here, the goal is to find the specific object that meets a given pattern rule. In a scene with many pieces of furniture, the computer may try to find the chair, for example. It would do this by starting with the rules for chair and by finding which objects in the scene satisfy these rules.

3. *Feature extraction:* This is a process that allows the computer to list, usually numerically, the various features of the object or objects it views. In a room of furniture, for example, the IU system might extract features such as the number of legs, the number of broad surfaces, the number of spherical surfaces, and so on. This process makes matching or classification easier because computation is greatly facilitated when facts are represented numerically. In the room of furniture, a chair may be recognized as having two legs, two broad surfaces, four right angles, and so on. This process of quantifying a scene can be performed on even very complex scenes.

Visual Characteristics into Whole Images

Once the IU system has extracted and quantified the features (or it has at least represented them in computable form), it usually plots them along a graph called a *feature space.* A graph of the features of a chair could be devised with the number of broad surfaces on one axis, the number of right angles on another, and the number of uprights on a third (many dimensions can be represented on a computer graph). Any item that is located at the junction of the three axes would be described as a chair.

The Region Method

Feature spaces are useful in classifying objects even when the features of the objects do not exactly match the expected pattern. A chair, after all, might not have exactly the same features as a typical chair. The feature space handles this by dividing the graph into *regions*. An object need not fall exactly on the interesection of all the axes that represent a chair to be classified as a chair. The object would just have to fall in the region of these axes. The parameters of the region would be determined by the programmer.

For example, we may define the angle the back of the chair makes with the seat to be between 85 and 135 degrees. But suppose a designer invents a chair that reclines more than 135 degrees or that even tilts forward more than 85 degrees. That chair might fit the other pattern rules while lacking just this one. On the graph, the chair would fall very near the correct axes, but it would not fall dead center. But as it would fall within the chair region, the system would categorize it as a chair.

Using this region method may on occasion cause objects to be misidentified. The system is not free of errors. This is one of the problems with artificially intelligent machines in general. The decisions generated by such systems may not be correct as often as those generated by conventionally programmed computers. But the programs can be used in many ways that would be impossible with conventional programs. The program may occasionally have to resort to such indecisive output as "probably a chair." But this kind of response is the one we might expect from a human confronting the same visual image.

If, as is rarely the case, the feature space were made up of only two axes, the regions could be separated by a series of straight lines. However, because most regions have to be defined in multidimensional space, a more complicated divider called a *hyperplane* is used to separate the regions. Hyperplanes are theoretical lines represented by mathematical formulas that exist in models with more than two dimensions.

The Prototype Point Method

An alternative to the region method is the *prototype point* method, which uses a graph point at which the axes of all the features of a general example of the object meet. When the IU system senses an object, it extracts features of the object and plots them on the feature space graph. If the object corresponds exactly to this prototype point, the object would of course be categorized accordingly; if it does not correspond to any point exactly, the IU system would categorize it as the object that it most nearly resembles.

The Template Method

Another approach to categorizing objects is to use the *template* method. In an IU system, a template is a series of numbers generated during feature extraction. In this method, however, a graph is not generated. Instead, each number is located and obtained separately. For example, there might be a category for the height of the object, another for the number of legs, and so on. When a new object is sensed, it is compared feature by feature with the template object in the computer memory. The object would have to match exactly the features in the template a given number of times to be categorized as a match with the template object. Characteristics that are more important than others— a chair, for example, has to have at least a back support if it is not to be considered a stool or a bed—are given more weight. Template matching has been found useful with objects, such as typed letters, that are limited in variety.

Technical Aspects of Image Recognition and Processing

Television cameras usually give information to IU systems. The image received from the camera is divided into a series of tiny segments—perhaps 500 or more. Each segment is then rated with a number representing the brightness of the segment. The image is thus entered and stored in computer memory as a series of numbers corresponding to the brightness of various points on the screen.

Before a computer can perform IU functions with this data, it must make a primal sketch of the image it is viewing. A primal sketch is similar to an outline drawing of the scene. Significant lines, such as edges around objects, are drawn. But insigificant lines, such as shadows, cracks, and creases—anything that might confuse the system and cause an object to be incorrectly classified—are eliminated.

The first step in generating this primal sketch is to eliminate areas of excessive brightness or dullness, areas that would throw off classification of the objects in the scene. Light bouncing off a pen might cast an area of high illumination across a man's body, for example. If this line of light were allowed to remain, the computer might interpret it as a significant edge, and the image of the man would be cut in two. Even one or two tiny dots of distorted illumination could cause problems for computer programs. These areas are called *noise,* and the process of eliminating noise is called *smoothing.* There are many methods of smoothing, but they all function according to the general principle that a point that is a certain number of degrees higher (or lower) than neighboring points is adjusted downward (or upward) according to some formula.

Once an image is smoothed, it is represented to the computer as a list of numbers, such as the following:

1 1 1 3 3 4 4 4 6 6 6 3 3 2 2 1 1

The computer now has a series of numbers representing the brightness of various points on the scene. However, the variations of brightness are only useful if the computer were attempting to generate an exact representation of the scene with all the shades of gray. But what is needed to generate a primal sketch is elimination of middle tones and discovery of sharper edge tones. To do this, the computer needs a series of numbers signifying the changes in the brightness of each point. This is because, after smoothing, any change in brightness should signify an edge.

We therefore want to generate a new list of numbers showing not the brightness of each point, but the change in the brightness of each point as compared to an adjacent point. The formula for accomplishing this is:

NEW NUMBER = OLD NUMBER–NUMBER TO LEFT OF OLD NUMBER

It works with the list above in the following manner.

The first number (1) is ignored because there is no number to the left. The second number is also 1. The NEW NUMBER for the second 1 is found by subtracting the number to the left (1), which results in 0. The 0 means that there is no change between a number and the preceding number. This would signify that no edge exists. The complete new list would be as follows:

0 0 2 2 1 1 1 2 2 2 −3 −3 −1 −2 −1 −1

We have thus generated a list not of the brightness of the scene but of the changes in brightness. The larger the change in brightness, the more likely that an edge exists. This is the first step in generating the primal sketch.

Using this information, the computer begins to generate the primal sketch. When a gap is found, the computer uses certain rules to determine the logical continuation of the line or curve until it meets up with another edge (for example, all edges must form corners with other edges).

Forming the primal sketch can be done by concentrating on regions rather than on lines and curves that surround regions. This type of program would not look at large differences in brightness but would recognize large areas of the same brightness. These areas would be considered one region. Each region would then be surrounded by a line or curve in the primal sketch.

Regions are also composed of areas of similar texture. A texture is a pattern. Each region of the same texture can be surrounded with a line or curve as well.

We will now look more closely at how various IU programs determine how to join the lines and shapes to form objects.

Broad Partitioning

An early AI program was able to divide a scene into broad partitions that delineate the possible different objects in the scene. For example, in the following figure we see what most likely is one block sitting on top of another. One block is made up of sides A, B, and C; the other is made up of D and E. The program is able to understand which sides belong to which block by analyzing the links in the picture. A *link* is where lines meet; this junction tends to occur when two shapes belong to the same object. The figure shows some examples of links. Areas labeled with a plus sign are likely to be part of the same object.

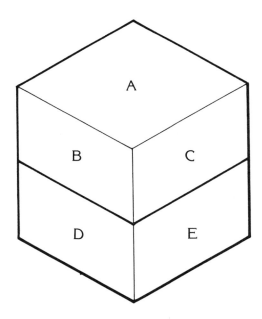

The program goes through the scene twice. First, it generates a list of the links that are formed for each broad surface. Note that the arrow link indicates that inside areas should be considered as one object. The fork links imply that all three areas belong together.

The following figure shows the links found in our block drawing:

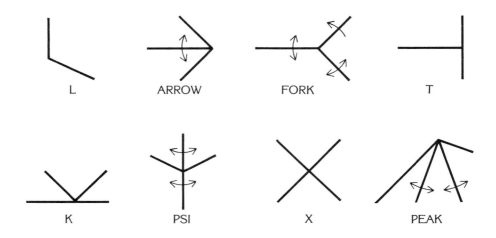

Shadows

Dealing with shadows is both a problem and an aid for scene analysis programs. The problem is in the possibility that the program will mistake the shadow for a broad surface. This could lead to false links being formed. The problem is partly solved by forming a theory of shadow links. It was found, for example, that shadows could be recognized by the fact that they form two or more L-type links in a row.

Once shadows are discovered, they can provide clues to the makeup of the scene. In the following figure, for example, there is no way of knowing if the block is floating, sitting on a narrow surface, or sitting

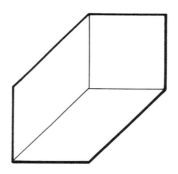

on a broad surface. If a shadow were formed a lot of information about the surface could be discovered. For example, a long shadow that does not curve is evidence of a surface that is straight for at least the length of the shadow. If the shadow curves, there is an edge on the surface at that point.

Suppression Using Physical Constraint Analysis

It is sometimes necessary not to assume that broad surfaces should be joined. Things such as cracks and seams will often confuse an image-understanding program. One way to solve this problem is to take into account that certain shapes cannot exist in the real world. Many rules about the relationships between junctions and the planes they join have been developed. These rules show that some of these junctions are impossible. The following figure is an example of an "impossible" object. Programs have been developed to automatically discount any junction that, when it joins two planes, forms an impossible object.

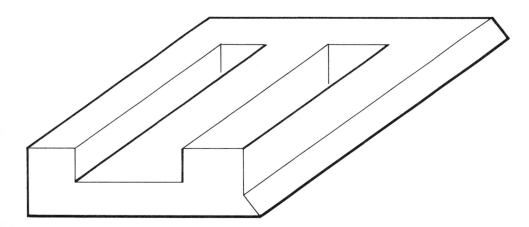

Relationship between Objects

Often, a complete picture can be discovered by understanding the relationship between primitive shapes. For example, we can view the world partly as a combination of bricks and wedges. The relationships that can exist among these are above, supports, in front of, right of, left of, and face to face (that is, with a common edge). If, for example, you have three blocks, two resting on a table and supporting one above (as in the next figure), the knowledge that the supporting blocks are related to the one above (they support it) provides information about their sides, which are hidden from view. We know that the tops of blocks A and B must not be completely open; if they were, C would not be supported.

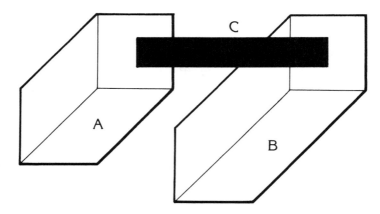

Object Function

A recent idea is to program the IU system to reason about the probable uses of objects and to use this information as a clue to the identity of the object.

For example, cups come in many different shapes and sizes. When humans see a cup shaped slightly differently from any they had seen before, they would probably have little trouble identifying it. This is because they would think about the probable use of the object. Programming this knowledge into the computer eliminates the task of having to include in the data base an image of every conceivable type of cup.

There are three possible functional descriptions of a cup:

1. It can be lifted.
2. It can contain liquid within it.
3. It will not topple over when placed on a flat surface.

Such a definition will work for almost any cup. The computer discovers these functions through the following rules about functions:

1. A thing that is small probably can be lifted.
2. A thing that is hollow and that has openings at one end can contain liquid.
3. A thing that has a flat bottom will not topple over when placed on a flat surface.

All vision programs thus far developed or presently being developed involve understanding images within a narrow range of possibilities. No system can view objects at random in an unstructured environment and identify them. This task is, unfortunately, far removed from current capability.

One researcher, William Richards, has offered one possible way to provide a computer with the ability to identify objects at random. His paper entitled "How to Play Twenty Questions with Nature and Win"[6] describes the process of identifying just one characteristic of an object viewed in an unstructured environment: whether the object is a mineral, an animal, or a vegetable. The process is similar to that used in the game of Twenty Questions, in which the questioner, by asking twenty questions, tries to guess what someone is thinking. The program would consider questions such as: Is the object moving? How many supports does it have? What acoustical frequencies are emitted? What is the acoustic source? And so on. Each answer carries with it a weighted score that leads to a classification of the object as animal, vegetable, or mineral. The paper is particularly interesting in that all answers can be discovered using presently existing devices. Obviously, narrowing the object down still further would require many more questions. However, the idea provides one possible solution to the problem of identification.

Image-understanding systems seem to have more problems in attempting to equal human behavior than most other AI projects do. This is because, in using vision, humans make more assumptions than in almost any other area of intelligent activity. When we look at something, we almost never see a complete object. Most usually, we are confronted with one or two sides of an object—and these are usually partially obscured. And yet, even young children, and most probably some animals, are able to make correct assumptions about the invisible sides. Psychologists have proved that in many cases a human can fill in a scene when given only the most rudimentary outline of the scene. In fact, humans have a need to invent scenes from images, as in our tendency to "see" reasonable scenes in abstract painting or in ink blots.

There are many aspects of human image understanding that are not fully understood. And there are problems (i.e., illusions) for which humans must compensate by using other areas of the intellect. The rest of this chapter will deal with those functions of the human image-understanding apparatus that are particularly difficult to program into a computer.

UNPROGRAMMABLE PROCESSES?

Human image processing is very fast partly because of the large number of parallel sensors that transmit information from the eye to the brain (10^6 by one count). You can easily understand the advantage of parallel processing by comparing the number of sensory inputs that the eye can relate at one time with the very limited number of inputs processed at a time by the ear (a sequential processor).

This speedy processing primarily involves recognizing objects and distinguishing them from their surroundings. But this is not all that happens almost simultaneously and automatically. The approximate size of objects is determined, the shapes of unseen backs and sides are surmised, and relative speed is approximated. These approximations and guesses are correct enough for humans to "trust their eyes" more than, say, their ears. But mistakes do occur. Some of these errors are caused by malfunctioning of the machine apparatus because of the influence of drugs, fatigue, dizziness, and so forth. Other errors result from logical difficulties that stem from the nature of the subject of the perception. These difficulties, called optical illusions, are also likely to present problems for machines built to mimic human image understanding.

Part of the problem with building seeing machines is related to the problem of developing a manageable data base as large and efficient as the human brain. This data base contains not only information about objects, but also rules for making assumptions about parts of objects that we cannot see. For example, when we see a chair from one angle and recognize the chair immediately, we are using this data base more than we are using our optical nerves. What we actually see is probably one or two rectangles and maybe a leg or two. We match this incomplete picture up with images in our data base and make certain assumptions about the parts of the object that we cannot see. If we see only two legs, and if the chair is not tipping over, we assume that there are two other legs. We also assume other characteristics of "chairness"—for example, the ability to support a sitter and the inability to fly. We also reject, for as long as possible, information about the chair that does not fit our expectations. For example, a chair that is built with only two front legs (but that is supported through a system of weights) would be seen by most quick glancers as also having rear legs.

Our ability to fill in features extends to extreme lengths. In a cartoon, for example, a few lines may represent a face. Viewers who are later asked to recall the face will "remember" features that were not actually present.

Psychologists have even questioned how much of each image is actually transmitted from the retina to the nervous system. It is known, for example, that frogs perceive only movement, edges, and intensity of light. From this rudimentary knowledge, they receive a total impression of the world, or an impression that is enough for hunting, eating, mating, and eluding predators. It has been suggested that the human retina may in some cases transmit only those same qualities to the brain. Whether this is true or not, what is certain is that perception is not accomplished simply by transmitting and then matching images.

The distance of an object is approximated through the richness or fuzziness of images, through the haziness of the intervening atmosphere, through the size, and through the knowledge that closer objects block further objects from sight. These aids to determining distance can easily be fooled, though, especially when one of the clues is distorted (a toy car may be used as a full-size car in a movie set, for example).

In general, the shrinking of retinal images is seen by humans as the distancing of an object. This does not work well in photography (even motion photography), in which miniature objects can easily masquerade as full-size objects. These illusions create special problems for machines that must depend entirely on photographic images for input.

Many researchers assume that the most economical way to build an image-understanding machine is to allow the machine to learn and understand new images as it comes across them. Present-day vision machines are built with specific applications in mind. They are therefore very specialized and unable to function in most real-world situations. They cannot learn new applications, even those that are very close to the application for which they were built.

But the problem with building image-understanding machines that are able to learn is that humans, the models for such machines, do not learn to accept new images well. In one experiment, human subjects were asked to stand in a room with non-standard wall lengths. As a result of this distortion, a child at one end of the room appeared larger than an adult standing at the other end of the room. (Both child and adult were viewed by the subjects in correct perspective before the experiment.) The subjects would have to "see" the child as being larger than the adult or would have to learn that a room can exist with irregular walls. In almost every case, American subjects could not see the child and adult correctly. Zulu subjects, however, not used to rectangular rooms, were able to perceive the situation correctly. You can see that even human perception systems cannot adapt well to new environments. How then can machines be built to do so?

One human capability that has not as yet been programmed into a machine is the ability to use prediction in perception. We drive along a road at night, and the glare of oncoming headlights temporarily blinds us. Yet we can continue to move safely for a few seconds and to remain on the road. We are able to perceive the road from memory. We can also guess about what other drivers are likely to do and "see" them doing those things during our temporary blindness. In a factory, a bolt may bounce off an object and fly straight up in the air. Although we may lose sight of the bolt, we perceive it is above our heads and that it threatens to hit us, so we act accordingly. Machines must also be able to perceive the existence of objects that temporarily move out of sight.

Many problems in human perception are also likely to trouble a machine. For example, there is the optical illusion called the "waterfall effect." People who view movement in one direction for a long period of time will often "see" movement in the opposite direction after the original movement ceases. This occurs even when another important clue to movement, change of scene, is absent. We "see" a physical impossibility, and yet we accept it. The illusion might arise because of a rule of thumb that humans unconsciously use in order to save time: Movement, once commenced, will continue for some time; therefore, to check repeatedly if movement is continuing is not necessary. Because the continuance of movement is not checked regularly, cessation of movement is not detected right away. It is likely that machines will have to process information in a similar manner and will have to "live with" similar paradoxes.

Human perception systems, then, depend only partly on the sensory apparatus. Therefore, the human system may make errors in understanding the objective world. But the trade-off is that it can perceive more than it would if it "played it safe" and never "saw" anything more than the information received through the eyes.

Machines that perceive will eventually require similar capabilities. Although research in this area continues, present-day IU systems are programmed to take a more careful (and therefore more limited) view of the world.

▪ 6 ▪

Robotic Systems

Few things excite people about technology more than the thought of robots working around the home and office. Both in science fiction and in reality, robots seem to be the one area of artificial intelligence that has captured the imagination of the general public.

Present-day robots, though, are far from the intelligent creations that are portrayed in *Flash Gordon* and *2001: A Space Odyssey*. They are slow, clumsy, stupid, and mostly blind. But even these Neanderthal precursors to a more intelligent race are already playing a major part in the manufacture of autos, farm equipment, and other products.

APPLICATIONS OF ROBOTIC SYSTEMS

Present-day robots are found primarily in manufacturing because factory tasks originally designed for automatic tooling machines and repetitive assembly-line operations can make good use of current state-of-the-art robotics. Robots today have extremely limited vision (at best), no "touch" functions, and very restricted movement. But these failings do not present much of a problem in a repetitive and structured manufacturing environment. And implementation of robotic technology in a factory almost always results in substantial productivity increases.

But these gains in productivity are just the tip of the iceberg. Factories of the future will have robots and intelligent machines controlling most operations from planning to packing.

In these plants, computer-aided design (CAD) will make the designing process easier and quicker. (CAD is a process in which a draftsman designs a product on a computer screen). Computer-aided manufacturing (CAM) machines will transmit the design to robots and other machines that are used in the manufacturing process. Computer-aided process planning will route materials through the factory floor and will instruct robots to be at correct locations at correct times. Computerized production planning and scheduling will order parts and distribute them throughout the factory. Robots will pick parts from stockrooms and receiving rooms and will place them in robot distributors, which will carry them around the plant. Robot assembly systems will receive these parts and will assemble the entire product. Robot quality-control systems will make measurements and will check fittings. And robot managers will report on the progress of all aspects of the process to the one human supervisor.

All these functions are now available in some form and are becoming more and more sophisticated. Japanese manufacturers already have at least one showcase factory that is manned by only one human and that is worked exclusively by robots during some shifts. Using robots allows a factory to run four 40-hour shifts a week and still leave eight hours for maintenance. Even the busiest non-robotic factories can manage only three shifts a week. And the graveyard shift usually requires differential pay.

Time-study engineers have proved that an eight-hour shift usually translates into only five to six hours of peak work. A well-maintained robot can work at peak efficiency for an entire shift—without breaking or slowing down.

Once robotic manufacturing is implemented, using human labor will seem very impractical. Humans need so many facilities that are irrelevant to the manufacturing process: They need washrooms and use tons of water; they need air conditioning in the summer and excessive heat in the winter; they need parking spaces, cafeterias, telephones, medical benefits, and a large number of supervisors. As working machines, humans are singularly ill-suited for repetitive manufacturing jobs.

Cost Factors

Although current robots are more limited in their uses than robots that will exist in the future, this in itself does not explain the slowness that manufacturers have exhibited in employing this technology. Economics is the important consideration. Robots still cost from $100,000 to $250,000, and these figures include only hardware. Robots also have to be programmed. Economic factors, combined with present-day use limitations, have resulted in a less-than-open reception by many manufacturers.

Japanese manufacturers, though, have committed themselves more completely to robot technology. The Japanese government has invested hundreds of millions of dollars in research and development of robotically controlled and operated factories. And, partly as a result of this, the Japanese are able to produce in some cases twice as many products each man-hour as manufacturers in the United States.

But the question of whether the expense of automating a factory is cost-effective (considering the enormous capital investment) may soon become moot as the cost of robots drops. High prices represent in part the high cost of research and development. Once this is written off, robots that use technology already established and paid for will become dramatically less expensive. This will be true of the hardware and especially true of the software (the cost of which almost entirely involves R & D expenses).

Another factor that will reduce costs is the more extensive use of robots in the robot-building process. Today, robot manufacturers use robots in only a few assembly operations. As robot manufacturers themselves will be among the first manufacturers to make use of state-of-the-art robotics, this probably will reduce the cost of robots and make them more feasible even for middle-size companies.

Robots are built primarily with expensive metals. But manufacturers are beginning to work more with less-expensive, injection-molded plastics in robotic production. This material is not only less expensive than metal, but it also makes possible the movement of robot parts by pressurized water, a process that tends to lower maintenance costs.

Robots in Construction

Another use of robots will be in the construction trade. Robots virtually do not exist in construction now primarily because of their lack of mobility. A robot carpenter or steelworker would have to be able to travel in and out of building sites littered with debris, creased with ruts, and outfitted with doors, stairs, and other obstacles.

Although the problems of robot locomotion are far from being worked out, the physical form that robots will have has already been developed: Cherry pickers, cranes, forklifts and other machinery are outfitted with wheels and tractor assemblies that allow locomotion in very difficult terrain. Once these machines arrive at their destinations, their legs will extend to serve as a stabilizing base. This type of locomotion and stabilization will form the basis of many construction robots.

But there are many more problems to solve besides locomotion before robots can be used in the construction trades. The biggest problem is that of building adequate image-understanding systems. Current systems are crude, and even those on the drawing boards will not be able to sense exactly where to dig a hole or where to drive a nail. Human painters and backhoe operators constantly use their eyes to get feedback to check how close they are to the mark. Construction robots will need vision systems that allow images to be constantly entered so that the machines can constantly rectify their positions.

Construction robots must also be able to deal with the unexpected and the unusual. Human carpenters know how to drive nails to avoid electrical boxes; crane operators can react quickly to a beam that seems a bit shaky. A construction robot has to be able to act quickly and intelligently in emergency situations in an environment that is a lot less controlled than the factory floor.

Another problem is that construction workers are better trained than factory workers. Construction workers' jobs are more varied and require more acts of judgment. A factory worker may turn a screw or weld one part eight hours a day, but a carpenter will rarely spend the entire day nailing boards.

These problems can be solved, but they require the use of technology that we are only beginning to develop. Vision and touch (sensory) systems have to be perfected along with decision-making programs. Force sensors must be implemented to enable a robot to use just the force necessary to complete a job, but not so much force as to break the material with which it is working. The actual process of construction might have to be altered to accommodate robots. The amount of debris at construction sites will have to be reduced, barriers such as doors and gates may have to be altered (or installation of these may have to be delayed until robots complete their work) and the process of nailing, digging, welding, and so forth may have to become more structured and proceed in a more routine manner.

Robots in the Home

Using robots in the home will present many of the same problems found in construction. Homes have at least as much debris and as many obstacles as construction sites. And the landscape also changes often. Robots that vacuum, place dishes in a dishwasher, or set a table must not only be able to learn the locations of objects but also must be able to adjust to constant change. To be truly useful, these robots will need better perception and feedback systems than even those used in the construction trades. This is because most home-owners are unwilling to keep a house "robot-ready," whereas a construction foreman might be willing to do so if higher productivity were the result.

A final problem in the use of home robots is cost. Robots would have to be built with at least reasonable capabilities and with a purchase price of three or four thousand dollars before they will be able to enter most homes. In the last analysis, cost could be the most persistent problem with the implementation of the robot in the home.

Robots in Hazardous Environments

Another important use of robots will be in environments either where humans cannot go or where humans require expensive protective devices.

Robots can be used underwater; they would not have to return to the surface to refill oxygen tanks, and they would not have to be protected from compression and decompression problems. The structure of robots makes them very suitable for underwater work. They would be almost weightless, and their buoyancy could be governed by air being introduced or released. Their arms and legs and tools could be worked with water-powered jets, and water lubrication would be easy and automatic.

Robots could work in underwater mining. Using robots in this function would be safer and much cheaper than using humans. Also, underwater construction of bridges and tunnels and underwater cable-laying would be made much safer and less problematic.

Once the area under the oceans is opened to development, many uses only dreamed of could be implemented. For example, underwater farming (both of fish and plants) would become feasible, and underwater solar collectors could provide electricity for vast areas of the earth.

And finally, robots will enhance our use of the moon and perhaps of Mars. Any practical use of these unfriendly environments would require structures that, while almost as dexterous as humans, would not be susceptible to human frailties.

A lot of progress in creating image-understanding systems and AI programming must be made before robots can be used on a large scale. At the same time, however, every new discovery in AI research will be accompanied by the question "How can this be implemented in robotics?" This is because, of all AI machines and procedures, robotics is the one that can so readily and so dramatically change our world.

ROBOT PROGRAMMING

The advantage a robot has over a conventional automatic tooling machine is that one robot can perform many tasks while a tooling machine is limited to only one or at best a few functions. The versatility of the robot lies first in the machine's unspecialized, multifunctional hardware and second in the relative ease with which new functions can be programmed.

Teaching by Showing

The most common, although most primitive, method of programming a robot is called "teaching by showing." This technique involves "walking" the robot through tasks and noting the movements and the activation of machinery (such as welding machines) during the process. After the computer is guided through the process once, a program of joint movements and machine activations is generated.

This method of programming works well in processes in which there tend to be no contingencies. Spot welding, painting, and riveting, for example, are usually unconditional activities. Other activities, however, such as inspection and mechanical assembly, may require conditional loops in the program of the robot. The activities of the robot must be guided not only by prearranged instructions but also by sensory input, data retrieval, and computation.

Robot-Level Languages

Many robot systems are equipped with robot-level programming languages. These languages use commands that instruct the robot to extract data from sensors—such as vision or force sensors—and modify behavior based on the data it receives. This allows the robot to deal with different situations and allows the programmer and planner to eliminate the strict structuring of the work environment and functions of the robot.

The key drawback to robot-level languages is that they require on-hand programmers. A factory worker can guide a robot through a task and thus effectively program it, but programming a robot (or even making a flowchart for such a program) using computer commands requires a high level of skill and sophistication.

Task-Level (World-Modeling) Programming

A third approach to robot programming—one that is not yet in commercial use—is called task-level or world-modeling programming. Using this technique, a programmer prescribes goals for where objects should be at any point in the manufacturing process. This is combined with input about the work environment surrounding the objects being manipulated and with information about the geometry and functions of the robot itself. All this information forms the basis of the program.

In general, a robot must carry out three functions to assemble a part:

1. It uses its vision system to find the correct part.
2. It grasps and removes the part from the conveyer belt as the part rides by.
3. It either installs the part in the assembly or sets it aside for later use, depending on the state of completion of the assembly.

While these three steps describe the action in very general terms, actual programming requires much more specificity. For example, these are some of the programming steps the robot must follow to remove just one part from the conveyer belt and to screw it onto the assembly:

1. Using the vision system, it identifies the part as it passes by on the conveyer.
2. It inspects the part for defects, such as a missing screw hole.
3. It determines the position of the part relative to the robot.
4. It moves to the grasping position identified in step 3, taking into account the movement of the belt.
5. It grasps the part using programmed force.
6. It tests its grasp size to determine if it matches the expected grasp size of the part. If it does not, the robot signals a possible error in the vision system.
7. It places the part on the assembly using programmed force. Any twisting or screwing of the part would be programmed at this point.
8. It removes a screw from the screw feeder and lines the screw up with the expected location of the screw hole. The location of the screw hole is determined by the input location of the part.
9. It inserts the screw in the hole and turns using programmed force. Screwing ceases when a certain torque factor is reached.

The Importance of Sensory Information

The operation above requires three types of sensors:

1. *Position sensors:* These may be located in the conveyer belt as well as in the joints of the robot. They determine the relative positions of the part and of the grasping mechanism of the robot.

2. *Vision sensors:* These are not necessarily located on the robot it-self. More likely, they are located somewhere above the conveyer belt for two reasons—first, the position provides better vision and elimi-nates the need to program the robot to move into various "seeing" po-sitions; and second, the position of the camera above the assembly pro-cess allows the manufacturer to use the same vision system for other robots.

3. *Finger-touch sensors:* These control the magnitude of the gripping force and detect the presence or absence of an object in the grasp of the robot.

Clearly, sensors play a very important part in the programming of robot applications. Because of the expense involved both in sensor hardware and software, however, industrial robots use very few sens-ing devices. Hence, the work environment is arranged to eliminate spatial uncertainty. One way to do this is by using feeders rather than con-veyer belts to deliver parts to the grasp of the robot. The problem with feeders is similar to the problem with automatic tooling: Both require expensive machines that can be used for one operation only. Thus, the main advantage of using robots is eliminated.

The use of sensors is therefore essential if we are to take advantage of the versatility of robots. Sensing programs require first that input and output routines allow the robot to obtain information from the environ-ment, and second that the entered data control where in the program the robot goes next.

Sensors can be used to do four major tasks. They can stop and start motion, they can choose among alternative actions, they can identify objects, and they can alter actions depending on external constraints.

Of these four functions, the most common is that of starting and stopping robot actions. Almost every robot program has a mechanism that waits for an external signal that tells the robot to begin a routine. In using feeders, for example, the arm motion of the robot is usually triggered by passage of a part that breaks a light beam.

Start-and-stop action can also be used to locate an object. The ap-proach of a robot hand toward an object can be stopped when a mech-anism on the hand senses a predetermined force threshold. Repeating this action a number of times provides the robot with data from which it can determine the location of the object.

The second most important use of sensing programs is in choosing alternative actions. This function might be used in the inspection pro-cess, in which the robot chooses between placing a part in a fixture or in a disposal bin (depending on certain parameters—size, location of holes, and so forth). This function might also be used to determine if an action has produced a desired effect (for example, if the screwing of a screw resulted in the screw being tightened).

Determining the identity and position of objects almost always requires an IU system. Because of the complexity of such a system, it usually has its own processor. The robot then works with data received from the processor and computes the position of the object vis-à-vis its own position.

A robot constantly in motion must be able to respond to external stimuli. These external stimuli might include data entered from an IU system, information about force relayed from a torque detector on the hand of the robot, or even information from heat detectors or other analog devices. Most continuous motions that are not programmed must provide continuous feedback as to whether the action is producing the desired effect. Robot motion based on information received from external stimuli is called *compliant motion.*

Compliant robot movement requires that the coordinates of the task be computed either by the robot computer or by a processor to which the robot has access. One way to accomplish this is to provide the robot with a drawing of the part being worked on, but this task is tedious and prone to error.

An alternative is to allow the robot to discover (through tactile senses) the area to be worked on. However, a problem with this approach is that some of the material being worked on may be inaccessible to the hand of the robot.

Another method is to make use of information generated in the CAD process. This seems most promising, because it provides the robot with a complete picture of the material without the need for extra programming.

A fourth means of finding a specific coordinate on a fixture being worked on is light beams. Two cameras determine the location of a screw, for example, by determining the position, from two perspectives, of a light beam from a laser gun.

While these methods do give the robot system information about the location of a fixture, they do nothing to help the robot get to that fixture. In a tightly controlled environment, the motion of the robot toward a fixture might not be a problem. But in a constantly changing environment, specifying the location of an object is just not enough; the path of the robot toward that object must also be identified.

The path of the motion of a robot is represented by a series of many intermediate positions between the initial position and the final position. These intermediate positions are called *via points.*

In robot systems, these via points are preset. If, however, the programmer does not know the exact layout of the environment where an action will be done, he or she will define via points very conservatively, which thereby causes the robot to make a very large arc to avoid possible collisions (obviously resulting in undue slowness or redundancy of motion). This problem can be circumvented by defining the geometry of the materials in the environment and by defining functions in terms of necessary motions. By doing this, the robot could, say, arc weld with a slow, wide movement and pick up a block with a more direct, overhand movement.

The problems involved in coordinating motion in one robot are compounded when motion must be coordinated among two or more robots. When two robots are working on an assembly line, for example, one robot must know when the other has finished a task before starting its own. One way to accomplish this is to appoint one robot to be master. Before the other robot begins any motion, it queries the master as to whether it can begin the operation.

Another type of problem occurs when two robots perform a function simultaneously (e.g., two robots cooperate to lift a heavy box). Here both robots must lift exactly at the same time, or the majority of the weight would fall on one robot and possibly damage both the robot and the items being lifted. One solution is to have the robots perform the task in the same way humans would. The amount of force applied by the object tells the lifter if it is doing its share to carry the load.

As mentioned earlier, an alternative approach to robot-level programming is called task-level programming. If the robot is to place a screw in a hole using robot-level programming, that task must be defined by the many actions required of the robot to carry it out. In task-level programming, the only action called for is "PLACE SCREW IN HOLE."

As in computer languages of higher levels, task-level programs require interpreters called *task planners*, which translate the task-level languages into robot-level languages. A task planner requires information about the geometry of the parts in the robot environment, about the nature of tasks being carried out, and about plausible robot movements. Task planning will eventually be used with CAD/CAM systems.

ROBOT HANDS

More than any single part of the robot, sophisticated, dexterous hands can be instrumental in producing a versatile machine. Commercially available robots use *parallel jaw grippers:* two parallel blocks of metal. Usually, these grippers do not contain object or force sensors.

Robots are usually equipped with many different hands, each of which is used for a different function. Although multihanded robots work well at present speeds, changing hands for different activities will be frustratingly slow when the speed of robotic motion increases. And the cost of the hands, often as expensive as the entire assembly, can be prohibitive.

But even these special-purpose hands are barely sufficient for assembly tasks. In manufacturing certain parts, small incremental movements are necessary. Present-day hands have only about six degrees of freedom. To make incremental movements, the robot must have moveable joints. Most movement occurs in the large joints that are farthest from the tips of the fingers. Movement using these joints tends not to be precise. To imagine the difficulty in using such a hand, try turning a screw without bending your finger joints.

The solution to these problems is a dexterous, multipurpose hand with sensing capabilities. Although no such hand is yet commercially available, researchers have developed prototypes and commercial use is probably less than three or four years off.

Current research involves all aspects of hand design—from actuation to materials to sensing devices.

1. *Actuation:* To actuate a hand that has strength (for tightening screws) and a light touch (for delicate fingertip motion) is difficult. One possible solution is to use an electrohydraulic mechanism, the advantage of which is good strength without excessive weight. One problem with prototype electrohydraulic actuators occurs when small parts, such as fingertips, are manufactured—small valves are difficult to control (leakage rates approach full flow rates, and small valves are prone to contamination). Another candidate is the torque motor, which is more controllable. However, it is large and bulky relative to the strength it provides, although advances in this area are producing motors that are smaller and sacrifice only a small amount of strength.

2. *Transmission* (the means by which force is sent to manipulator joints): The challenge is to provide strength without sacrificing agility. Pulley chains and gears, while useful, tend to be bulky and not very flexible. Another problem is that extreme friction results from rapid movement of manipulator fingers and causes breakage. One researcher pointed out that in attempting to copy the human hand, developers have not yet been able to recreate what might be the most important ability, self-healing. Also, the lubricating system in the human hand has never been satisfactorily copied on a machine. One of the most promising ideas is the tendon tape transmission system. Tapes are used to contract and extend the fingers. The results of early experiments have showed that this system resists wear and exhibits good flexibility.

3. *Sensors:* Each hand must be equipped with sensors that can detect force, the presence of objects, heat, cold, and other conditions. The

most promising invention is touch-sensitive rubber material that can be slipped over the manipulator. This material alleviates the problem of wiring inside and shaping the sensor to fit the hand.

▪ 7 ▪

Teaching Systems

Although many AI researchers have expressed the hope and expectation that AI systems will be used in education, very few AI systems are being used in this way. Those that do exist, however, point the way to future progress in the field. Many AI programs that have been developed as educational aids have been scaled down to run in a much less powerful but adequate form on even small eight-bit computers. This chapter discusses some attempts to build computer-aided instruction (CAI) programs. Special emphasis is placed on PLATO programs and on the LOGO language, both of which are generally available in incarnations less powerful than the original.

Education consultant and computer scientist Cecily Resnick has pointed out that CAI programs fall into one of three categories:

1. Breaks down subject matter into small pieces. This courseware is similar to "programmed learning" books. Typically these programs interact very little with the student. Their main function is to move to the next exercise on command. Some people have called such programs "page turners" because they seem to be useful only in the sense that users don't have to turn pages. However, the programs often perform other functions, such as keeping test scores, finding averages, and so forth.

2. Interacts a bit more in that it directs the student to different aspects of study based on a limited number of factors. For example, some

programs will not allow a student to leave one test section until he or she answers a certain number of questions correctly. More sophisticated programs will determine the types of questions the student answers correctly or incorrectly and will use this information as criteria for choosing the subjects to explore further.

3. Understands the student's internal cognitive structures. These programs are able to analyze a student's answer to a question and determine which parts of the question confuse the student. They then use that information to provide very specific instruction. A system of this type would be a substitute for a very competent and experienced teacher.

Most programs for eight-bit computers are of the first type. Some programs made to run on larger computers, including most PLATO programs, are of the second type. Some PLATO-type programs, though, show some characteristics of the third type. If a computer is to act as a teacher in a manner similar to the way a robot acts as a factory worker, such a computer must be capable of performing as a type-3 system.

Another category of courseware closely linked to AI is the simulation programs. As we shall see, these programs provide a student with experience that is close to "real life" without the expense or, in some cases, the danger of field work.

The significance of a type-3 program is seen in the theories of Jean Piaget, the well-known educational psychologist. He pointed out that new knowledge is incorporated into a student's mind by fitting it into a predefined structure. This structure is the basis for the student's understanding of the world. If something does not fit into that structure, it is usually ignored. This is why, for some people, some things seem so difficult to learn while other concepts, often more complicated, may be easier to learn. A type-3 program can determine the incorrect structures that are confusing the student and can attack the structures directly—thus making the educational process more efficient.

PLATO

The University of Illinois at Urbana has conducted extensive research on learning systems. The result of this research is a system called PLATO. It uses a Control Data mainframe computer that provides a large memory, excellent graphics, and high speed (three to six thousand machine instructions per second). Most input is accomplished through a standard keyboard, but a panel allows users also to input by touching the screen. The panel senses touch in a 16-by-16 grid. Terminals have built-in computer-controlled slide projectors that can display onto the screens up to 256 images in a single microfiche. A high-fidelity audio device produces sound effects—a human voice, music, or real-world sounds for a simulation. The audio device can store up to four thousand separate messages, each up to 22 minutes in length.

Examples of PLATO programs follow. Some use AI techniques and philosophies extensively, some very little, but most use some form of heuristic search, problem solving, natural language, and other AI techniques.

Genetics
Prior to the introduction of the PLATO CAI system, University of Illinois students studied genetics by using fruit flies. Such experiments were difficult and expensive. A simulation program was developed; it stored genetic information in memory. When fruit flies are "mated" in the program, the computer generates an offspring composed of the characteristics randomly selected (in a statistically correct manner). A picture of the offspring appears on the screen.

Lunar Landing
More than simply an arcade game, this simulation includes equations of dynamics. The rocket reacts exactly as a real rocket would react in the lunar atmosphere.

Natural Language
Some PLATO programs allow student input (similar to NL input) in many different ways. Here is a brief example of an interaction in a chemistry class:

STUDENT: What color is it?
PLATO: The solid is white and the liquid is colorless.
STUDENT: What is its melting point?
PLATO: The melting point is 19–21°.
STUDENT: What does the nmr look like?
PLATO: This is the 60 MHz proton nmr spectrum. For a table of chemical shifts, press DATA. (The spectrum is shown on the screen.)
STUDENT: ir?
PLATO: This is the ir spectrum. (The inferred spectrum is displayed on the screen.)

Figure Recognition

PLATO can provide geometry lessons. It asks students to draw figures on the screen and intelligently copes with different sizes and angles of rotation of the geometric figures.

Lesson Planning

Human teachers must not only be proficient in imparting knowledge though lessons, they must also be able to plan lessons in such a way as to fit a particular student's work habits. For example, does the student work best when he or she begins with a difficult assignment or when he or she begins with an easy one? How much review is necessary? Should past work be reviewed before the main assignment? Should work be reviewed again, immediately after the main assignment? The lesson planner provides a lesson for a teacher-specified period of time. If the teacher specifies 30 minutes, for example, the planner will produce three slots of instruction. The amount of instruction in the lesson will be such that the student will use it for about 30 minutes. This computation is based on the average time most students take to perform the lesson and on the amount by which the student normally exceeds or falls short of this average.

Math Understanding

Many times a student's mistake in a math problem is based on a trivial misunderstanding of some part of the process. Rote practice may eventually dislodge this misunderstanding, but learning in this manner tends to be inefficient. Piaget pointed out that rote drills do not provide for a change in the internal structure that is often the cause of the mistake. Some educators put it another way: A child may be providing the correct answer to the wrong question rather than the wrong answer to the correct question. Math lessons programmed in PLATO attempt to discover what the student's misconceptions are. For example:

PLATO: $8 \times 8 =$
STUDENT: $8 \times 8 = 16$
PLATO: Did you mean to answer $8 \times 8 =$ or $8 + 8 = ?$

LOGO

The LOGO programming language now available in some form for most computers was developed at MIT to help children learn how to write AI programs. The most well-known part of LOGO is "Turtle

Graphics," or "Turtle Geometry." The "turtle" is actually a state that is made up of a screen position and a direction. It is most usually represented on the screen by a cursor. The turtle can be commanded to change its position or its heading through very simple statements. The turtle also has a "pen" so it can draw as it moves. Commanding the turtle to move will cause various shapes to be drawn on the screen.

Students can also prove theorems of turtle geometry. For example, in a theorem called "total turtle trip," the student proves that when a turtle makes a complete trip and ends up where it started, the total that it turned counterclockwise minus the total it turned clockwise is some multiple of 360 degrees.

LOGO can also be used by children in natural-language programming. Kenneth Kahn of MIT has developed LAIL, which stands for LOGO AI Language. According to Kahn, the program includes the following:

1. A powerful pattern matcher for natural-language understanding.
2. A sentence generator that structures sentences according to rules formulated by the child.
3. A relational data base for memory and inference.
4. An actor-like animation system (described below).

Although standard LOGO provides rudimentary animation, this capability is limited at best. Kahn's program is more advanced in animation. The animation is based loosely on the ACT programming language. An *actor* is an entity that receives messages and that can either act on those messages (i.e., carry out the command) or transmit the messages to another actor that has the capability of acting on them. In Kahn's system, each actor can accept turtle commands; each can act on the commands immediately, or remember them, or forward them; and each has a set of patterns programmed into it. Each actor matches received instructions against its programmed patterns. If a match is found, the actor associated with the command acts on it. An actor called a "scheduler" coordinates the activities of other actors that might be working simultaneously.

Here is how part of a program might be written:

SQUARE (MAKE GEORGE)   [A square is drawn and is given the name George.]
GEORGE (REMEMBER SPEED 25)   [George is to remember the speed of its movements.]
GEORGE (IF RECEIVE ZIGZAG ?N THEN ZIGZAG

GEORGE:?N)   [If George receives the command zigzag followed by a number, then it is to carry out the command.]
CIRCLE (MAKE SALLY)   [A circle is drawn and is given the name Sally.]
SALLY (DO FORWARD 100)   [Sally is told to go forward at a specific speed. Sally doesn't move yet because this information is being forwarded to the scheduler.]
GEORGE (DO ZIGZAG 75)
SCHEDULER (GO)   [The scheduler sends the messages that instruct Sally and George to begin their movements.]

The development of teaching systems has lagged behind that of their cousins, the expert systems, more because of economic realities than because of technical abilities. Educational institutions without funds to buy expensive programs are not as good customers as businesses that need expert systems are. But as in all areas of AI, knowledge gained in developing one system will easily be transferred to other types of systems.

· 8 ·

Distributed AI Systems

Distributed AI offers a means of solving problems affecting a large physical domain. Distributed AI comes into play in the coordination of the work of many robots in one factory. Another application is in the control of traffic that is spread across an area too large to be viewed by one sensor. These applications require that the different parts of the system be able to communicate and cooperate with one another.

In a paper published in AI Magazine,[7] Daniel D. Corkill and Victor R. Lesser listed three reasons that the study and implementation of distributed AI is both a possibility and a necessity for current AI research agendas:

1. Hardware technology has improved so as to make the building of large distributive networks not only possible but also feasible. This technology borrows heavily on distributive data processing (DDP) applications that allow remote terminals to communicate with mainframes. According to Corkill and Lesser, we are nearing a unique situation in which development of hardware technology has outpaced that of the problem-solving software necessary to utilize it.

2. As we shall see, a number of AI applications need distributive technology so as to succeed or at least to be made more efficient.

3. Understanding the process of cooperative problem solving is helpful in learning how to manage both humans and machines working in tandem.

Understanding the similarities and differences between DDP and distributed AI is important. The two technologies are similar in that the terminal the user is working on does not do all the processing. In DDP, the user might sit at a terminal to type in a problem; the computer will gain access to a mainframe or (less often) another terminal. An important difference between the two disciplines, however, is that DDP nodes gain access to other computers for very specific parts of a job, while distributed AI networks nodes act cooperatively to solve one single problem. If a user wants to receive the entire records of an employee through a DDP system, for example, he or she will ask for that information by typing on a terminal (which normally gains access to a mainframe, where the information is stored in a data base). In some DDP networks (or in local area networks), a terminal may gain access to another terminal, one that houses the needed information. For example, one terminal may contain medical records, another accident records, and so forth. The local terminal (or more precisely, the operating system) acts as a mailroom clerk who gathers and distributes information all over a corporation.

Each node in a distributed AI network, however, may work on a specific problem part in which it is an "expert." The problem part that each works on tends to be smaller than that in a DDP network. In general, AI network nodes work together more closely than those in a DDP network do.

DISTRIBUTED AI RESEARCH

The research in distributed AI also differs from other AI research in that problem-solving strategies are broken down into smaller parts. This requires that each node be equipped with a mechanism for dealing with the inability to solve a problem completely. Nodes, therefore, must be able to function at times with incomplete information. Nodes must also be able to store information until they receive instructions as to where to send it.

Distributive AI research has focused on those applications in which the nature of a problem requires an expansion of the problem-solving capability. Two applications that fit neatly into this category are automatic traffic control and distributed robot systems. In both, nodes must be able to perform local computing for many functions. But nodes also must be able to work with other nodes in planning routes that cross over two or more nodes. They must be able to plan how problem-solving work will be divided in each situation.

Sensors are also distributed in these two applications. In the traffic control system, for example, sensors are placed at various points along the road. This distribution decides which problem-solving applications should be performed locally (i.e., at one node) and which in cooperation (often necessary). Obviously, each node must be able to interpret scenes independently, because often an image will be picked up by one node only. (Each node must, for example, be able to monitor traffic in its area.) However, each node must also be able to send information about objects that will subsequently fall into the range of another node's sensor. This is essential, because individual nodes do not have information about the entire system. And, finally, there must be a way of determining which node will act on information that is culled from an image that appears at more than one node. The perceived object must not be considered two objects, and two or more nodes working on the same problem could sometimes be wasteful or even destructive to the network.

Making a Distributed AI System Work

As mentioned above, distributed AI systems must be able to function while being given only a partial understanding of a problem. A system that is able to function in this manner is a Functionally Accurate, Cooperative (FA/C) system. "Functionally accurate" means that the system will generate accurate—accurate to an acceptable degree—information based on input that may not always be accurate or complete. "Cooperative" refers to the activities of the nodes that send data to one another.

To see how an FA/C system works, we can look at a traffic-pattern monitor. The goal of the system is to generate an area-wide map of vehicles driving through a particular intersection. The system indicates the flow of traffic on a continuous basis. Each processing node in this system is associated with an acoustic sensor that has a limited range as well as limited accuracy, and the nodes are distributed over the area to be mapped. Each node communicates with nearby nodes by radio. This information is passed on, node to node, as a function of sound frequency. A processor at a higher level translates the information into symbolic language for processing.

As a vehicle moves through an area, its sound is picked up by various sensors within acoustic range. The information received by the sensors is limited and may also be inaccurate. Relying on information received from only one sensor can result in "seeing" vehicles that do not exist, not "seeing" vehicles that do exist, and incorrectly identifying the positions of vehicles. To correct this, information received from many sensors must be correlated over a specific period of time—each node confirming information received from the others.

If each node had to produce accurate and complete data before processing, the total input to the network would have to be distributed constantly to almost every node. Time, technology levels, and expense now make this practice infeasible. The alternative is to loosen the requirement that each node produce accurate results and to provide the means for each to work in an uncertain environment. A node could, for example, be required to produce as many alternative descriptions of the flow of traffic in its area as seem necessary, based on inconsistent incoming information. Or nodes could be given information about the statistically probable locations of vehicles. If a vehicle seems to be in two locations, the node will place it at the statistically probable location; or, if any two out of three "clues" detect a vehicle or point to one possible location, this information would be assumed to be correct. The goal is not to create a perfectly accurate map, but one that is statistically correct over a period of time. At any one time, however, there is the possibility of error.

PROBLEMS IN DISTRIBUTED AI DEVELOPMENT

Lesser's recent experiments with only three nodes point to some problems and needs for further distributed AI hardware and software development. The problems showed up not so much in lack of accuracy but in poor efficiency of the network. In some cases, a node that produced an accurate representation of a situation would not have the means to cease investigation and would continue to produce other (inaccurate) representations. In other cases, overly noisy input would prevent nodes from making hypotheses about situations, and the nodes would continue to produce improbable hypotheses.

The general problem lies in providing a local processor with the means for determining when it must "give up" searching for answers (either because it has given the correct response or because it has not received sufficient information). There is obviously a trade-off here: The more time a system spends attempting to be totally accurate, the more time it takes for each computation. But to limit computation time may limit accuracy beyond an acceptable level.

Lesser's experiments indicate other areas for further study. For example, should information be transmitted from node to node continually or only when requested? The problem of nodes being distracted by inaccurate or unnecessary input shows that, in some cases, receiving more information is a hindrance to efficiency. And a final area of study is how to build an efficient command hierarchy of the nodes.

Both the questions raised by these limited experiments and the success achieved with them have encouraged Corkill and Lesser to devise a testbed for the problem. A *testbed* is a simulation that consists of, in this case, the entire program minus the sensory input. Input is provided by the experimenters in the same incomplete and often erroneous manner in which the sensory apparatus works. Here are a few characteristics of the testbed:

1. Internode communication is subject to error.
2. Sensors can err in three ways: They can fail to detect signals; they can detect nonexistent signals; and they can misread signal locations.
3. Nodes, sensors and internode communication devices can temporarily fail to function at any time.

Although this testbed has, as of this writing, taken between 15 and 20 man-years to develop, results have not yet allowed for the creation of a comprehensive distributed AI system in the real world.

One important use of the testbed is in changing variables in the network to see how the change affects the network as a whole. One such variable is the voluntary or compulsory nature of node communication. In a voluntary setup, a sensor communicates with nodes only when certain parameters are met. In a compulsory setup, all information is transmitted all the time. And in a mixed setup, some communication is always occurring, and other information is transmitted when parameters are met. A second variable is whether each node is self-directed or is directed by another node (or by a central processor). And, finally, the level of the information passed on—complete hypotheses, raw data, and so forth—is a variable.

Distributed AI is necessary if a system is to function as a group of humans working together. Communication among humans is an important part of developing intelligence. Without communication, many advances of our intelligent civilization would not have occurred. Communication among machines is necessary not only so they can mimic this ability in humans, but also so they will not need a human monitor to direct distributed activities.

▪ 9 ▪

AI in the Macrocosm

AI researchers have speculated on how AI could be used to solve the large problems in civilized society. For example, researchers P.D. Klrolak and J.H. Nelson have suggested a number of these possible applications:

1. *Political Organization:* Political voting districts have often been drawn by the party in power in a manner that tends to keep the party in power. Segments of a society that are most likely to vote for the opposition are broken into small groups and are scattered among friendly districts, thus minimizing their effect at the polls. Recently, courts have required that political districts conform to natural social boundaries and that they be approximately equal in size. A number of heuristic programs have been developed to design these boundaries scientifically. For political reasons, many of these computer-drawn districts are not accepted, but eventually they will be impossible to be ignored. These programs are able to take into account much census information, including nationality, level of income, and so on.

2. *Location of Public Facilities:* The location of schools, fire departments, libraries, and other public buildings should not be decided haphazardly. Issues to be considered in making decisions include accessibility to public transportation, nearness to groups not likely to have personal transportation, access to highways, the relative security of an area, and so on. Heuristic programs have been developed to help designers plan public sections of urban areas.

3. *Garbage Pickup:* Garbage pickup routes were in many cases established years ago and may now be severely inefficient. Redesigning a large-city garbage route can be expensive and time-consuming if done by humans. Programs, however, have been able to effect a 50-percent reduction in garbage truck travel.

4. *School Bus Routing:* Organization of a fleet of school buses involves problems of which most people are unaware. Distance and economy of travel are only two criteria that must be considered. Most state laws provide for a maximum length of time any student can ride the bus. The bus must be able to stop and make all required turns safely, which often limits the size of the bus that can be used on some streets. For example, a larger school bus may not be able to negotiate a turn that is easy for a smaller bus. The development of heuristic programs has resulted in shorter overall travel of the entire fleet, a shorter longest route, and better distribution (more even loads) of passengers.

5. *Busing to Achieve Racial Integration:* The problems of scheduling busing for racial integration are the same as in the previous AI application, but achieving the goal of defacto integration is an added difficulty. The program is required to do more than simply assign students to obtain a well-proportioned racial mix; it must take into consideration budget constraints, time of student travel, reallocation of teachers, renovation of facilities where necessary, and finally, bus routes. In one program, the process is accomplished in the following steps:

a. The school board provides the raw data for the computer. The data base consists of information about the location and condition of various facilities, the number of teachers who are willing to relocate, the availability of buses, and so on. Pupil information, including information about ability and race, becomes part of a pupil-locator data file. The school board then defines the problem succinctly. For example, the board may request that the system group students in classes according to ability. The board also submits a list of constraints regarding maximum pupil travel time, court orders, and so on.

b. The computer offers a rudimentary solution. It first generates a plastic overlay for a map of the area. This overlay contains the computer's proposal as to which populations should attend which facilities to work best within the goals and restraints of the school committee.

c. The information provided by the computer allows the planning committee to decide in a general way on the best plan for organizing the district.

d. The computer takes the information provided by the planner to schedule bus routes and student and faculty assignments. "Impossible" situations—conflicting goals—are also highlighted.

According to Marvin Minsky,[8] a remotely manned society is a future application for AI. By using the technology of remote control, says Minsky, artificial intelligence can change the nature of human life. The goal, as he sees it, is to create mechanical hands that are intelligently controlled, versatile, and economical. He estimates the total cost of the project at about one billion dollars and the time needed to complete it at ten to twenty years. However, benefits would be realized during all those years, and the cost would be recovered along the way by improved productivity and health. These improvements will be felt in many areas, including:

1. *Energy:* Few people dispute the idea that nuclear energy has the potential to provide the world with electricity through inexpensive and, in many cases, renewable materials. The main problems concern plant safety and recycling of waste material. Maintenance is much more difficult in nuclear plants than in conventional plants because of the nature of the material. If maintenance could take place without shutting the plant down and without interrupting normal operations, it could be done on a more regular basis, as is done in other types of plants. Minsky cites other advantages in remotely manning a nuclear plant:

   a. *Safety:* No one would be exposed to radiation.
   b. *Theft:* The possible theft of plutonium and other radioactive material has received publicity recently. A few groups in the United States have even claimed to have fashioned nuclear weapons and have threatened to blow them up if demands were not met. That all such claims turned out to be false does not relieve many people of the fear that thieves could gain access to places where nuclear material is stored. A remotely manned plant would drastically reduce the number of people who would need to enter the plant. It would also monitor all activity on a continuous basis and report suspicious activity to human or machine guards.
   c. *Reliability:* Constant inspections would almost entirely eliminate breakdowns and shutdowns.
   d. *Integration:* Because machines can virtually eliminate the possibility of human error as well as improve maintenance and inspection, on-site waste storage, waste processing, and energy production could be combined.
   e. *Economy:* Because materials can be handled easily and cheaply, materials with shorter lives can be used.

2. *Undersea exploration and exploitation:* Most of the planet is ocean. The vast resources in the ocean remain unutilized or underutilized because of the expense and danger involved in working underwater. Even underwater "plants" such as oil-drilling facilities are plagued by dan-

ger. The reason is similar to that mentioned in connection with nuclear plants: The difficulty in maintaining such systems results in their being undermaintained. A remotely manned underwater facility would be safe, cheap, and productive; it could be used for mining, farming, fishing, and exploration.

3. *Mining:* Industrialization took place last century partly on the backs of miners who died young from the labor that was to produce cheap energy. Present-day workers will not put up with such brutal and unsafe conditions. Providing safety as well as the higher wages now demanded has caused the price of coal (and of other energy-related products) to soar. Gaining access to resources will be cheaper and quicker with remotely manned mines.

4. *Industrial production:* This is the area in which robots have the most influence; in the future, AI machines will play a most important role. The economic structure of the world will be affected by these changes, and poverty and drudgery may be eliminated. There is, of course, much improvement to be made in automatic equipment before we can reach the goals outlined here. Some of these improvements are mentioned below. But probably the greatest advance over present-day technology will be in machines that can program themselves. Each minute activity that we desire of today's machines requires hundreds of hours of programming time. The ability to tell a machine in simple English what it is to do will provide the basis of the next industrial revolution.

Transportation, farming, education, and distribution of resources also will experience tremendous advances. In fact, few aspects of economic life will not be affected.

Minsky points out that the expense of one billion dollars is not high at all when compared with that of the research and development of much less complex and useful products. Spread over two decades, the cost of remotely manned plants will be about fifty million dollars a year. Redesigning one car model costs well over one million dollars. The design for one nuclear power plant costs much more.

Minsky estimates that it will take ten years to develop basic instruments. The next ten years will be used to refine and adapt these instruments to specific purposes.

MACHINES WITH HANDS

The main device that will accomplish all this is called a "telepresence" system, hands that will be as agile as a human's and that will be able to sense as well as a human hand and eye can. Existing devices that may be prototypes for such hands are the following:

1. *Force detectors:* These systems can determine the amount of force or resistance acting on the working part of a hand. This information can affect further machine actions.

2. *Computer control:* Systems are already controlled by computer programs. Activities such as directing the flow of tools and managing operations are automated.

3. *Robotics:* As seen in Chapter 5, some robots will develop into versatile mechanical servants.

According to Minsky, further work on mechanical hands will likely concentrate on the following:

1. *Flexibility:* Hands have very little ease of movement.

2. *Control systems:* Although today's system is controlled by the same program (CAD/CAM) that designs the product, the amount of control exercised by a computer is very limited. Usually, only the equipment flow and the cutting patterns are determined by the computer. Systems in the future will act as robot foremen in the making of more immediate decisions.

3. *Sensing:* Modern equipment has little or no sensing. Machines that are so equipped are able to recognize only a few patterns. Equipment of the future must be able to receive and act on sensory information as well as or better than a human can.

4. *General structure of the machine:* In general, the machine would probably be built to resemble a human—two arms (each with a shoulder), elbows and wrists, and five fingers on each hand; legs and feet will allow the robot to move in a littered environment. Some special-purpose machinery would allow the system to work in ways that would be difficult for humans to work in—such as in cramped spaces, in situations that require balancing on one leg, and so on.

To date, there is no centrally organized project to develop these and other AI systems in this country. All work is being done by university and business groups. The Japanese, however, have embarked on a ten-year centralized plan to develop strong AI technology. This project is discussed in the next chapter.

· 10 ·

The Japanese Fifth-Generation Project

In October 1981, the Japanese announced their plans to become the world's leading supplier of computers by the early 1990s. They will accomplish this, contend Japanese business people, by producing new types of machines. They claim that these new machines, called fifth-generation computers (actually AI machines), will change all aspects of human life for the better. Medicine, education, science, and industry will all be affected by fifth-generation machines in a way not experienced with any other technology before.

The initial cost of the project, $450 million, is not high by Western standards. What is important is that the funds are coming initially from the government. This ensures that the project will be centralized, planned, more efficient, and more likely to succeed than the dozens of fragmented areas of research in the United States.

The fifth-generation project effort is equivalent to the American space project. But there are big differences. First, little commercial use has been made of space; the fifth-generation project is admittedly commercial in its goals. Second, the space project does not provide much technical information to private industry; the fifth-generation project borrows industry scientists with the understanding that they will report back to their companies the information gained from their work.

At present, the United States is far ahead of the Japanese in AI technology and in computer technology in general. The admitted goal of many Japanese business people has always been to keep up with the large Western companies, especially IBM. The significant difference with the fifth-generation project is that this goal has been changed—no longer is it to keep a close second and to borrow American technology; the Japanese are now developing their own technologies. If successful, fifth-generation machines will be qualitatively different from any American precedent.

PROJECT BACKGROUND

In April 1982, the Japanese Institute for New Generation Computer Technology (ICOT) was established to guide the fifth-generation project. Its first plan of action is to develop an evaluation process that will allow project workers to measure their progress continually against their expectations.

Although the initial money for ICOT was provided by the government, eight private firms will be providing additional funding (estimated at a minimum of one billion dollars). The firms are Fujitsu, Hitachi, Nippon Electric Corporation, Mitsubishi, Mitsushita, Oki, Sharp, and Toshiba. These firms have contributed computer scientists to the project. Scientists have also come from two national laboratories, Nippon Telephone and Telegraph's Musashino Laboratories and the Electrotechnical Laboratory of the Ministry of International Trade and Industry (MITI).

The government agency that brought the fifth-generation project into being was MITI. MITI is an agency the purpose of which does not have an exact equivalent in the United States. Its purpose is to help businesses by determining what their best interests are and then to encourage them to conform to practices that will serve these interests. One reason MITI has been successful is that most Japanese companies realize that conforming is in their long-term best interests, even though doing so might require initial sacrifices.

An example of a MITI action occurred in the 1970s, when salaries began to rise in Japan. MITI began a voluntary plan that led many businesses away from labor-intensive manufacturing and into the industries that used less labor but that required higher levels of technology. The increases in technology that this action generated were brought about by the advances in the car and home-electronics industries. These advances allowed Japan to become a leading supplier of these products. The same project brought about new automated tooling and robotic system technologies, which have increased Japanese productivity in smokestack industries to the point that similar American companies are having serious problems keeping pace.

By the end of the 1970s, these successes encouraged MITI to look to other areas in which Japan would be able to excel. That the computer industry became the target is not a surprise, given the current computer explosion. What may be a surprise, though, is that MITI was not interested in developing better systems (e.g., in beating IBM). The goal of equaling or beating IBM had been that of many Japanese companies, but MITI wanted something new and different. It wanted something that was worth large-scale MITI involvement. It decided to leave the 1980s to the West and to those Japanese companies that wanted to continue their struggle. The new goal was to develop a system for the 1990s. The Japanese would not give up completely on the 1980s, but the big push would be aimed at the next decade.

In 1978, MITI asked the the Electrotechnical Laboratory to prepare a report on what the nature of these 1990 computers should be. The report was accepted, and by April 1982 the money was appropriated. Within a month, forty scientists were recruited and were housed in a Tokyo office. Work began.

The project has been supported financially during the first three risky years entirely through ICOT funds. And during the first year, all the work was done at ICOT. But by the second year, work was partially parceled out to the supporting companies on a contract basis. And all through the project, the researchers return regularly to their companies to discuss progress. There are no secrets at this point. And no profits are expected until the work moves to private hands.

GOALS OF THE FIFTH-GENERATION PROJECT

The technology that the Japanese intend to develop in the fifth-generation project is formidable. As opposed to U.S. AI developers, who tend to stress software development, the Japanese are placing a larger emphasis on hardware. One example of this is in system architecture. The standard architecture for computers is called *von Norman architecture,* named for a mathematician who helped to develop it. In this system, processing is done by a single CPU. All calculations are performed one at a time. By convention, computer speed is measured by how many million calculations the system can perform in one second. One million calculations are called a *megaflop.* Some large computers today can perform up to two megaflops.

This speed, while adequate for most scientific and business applications, is too slow for handling the gigantic data bases that could be at the center of AI systems. AI systems require *parallel processing.* The few experimental machines that can perform parallel processing are capable of much faster work. Multiple chips divide up each operation so that different portions of the problem can be solved simultaneously— that is, in parallel. Using this method, some machines have been said to run at eight hundred megaflops when performing simple mathematical calculations. This speed has never been fully tested, though, because programs have not yet been developed that can allow for more than twenty megaflops.

The most advanced parallel processing architecture proposed, but not yet built, is called *dataflow*. In this architecture, the computer is made up of a large number of small processors, each of which contains only a minimum amount of memory. The central processor is not used at all in the initial stage of solving a problem. Rather, each small processor communicates with one another in a complex network. The work is divided up according to specialties among the various processors. When all work is completed, each processor dumps the result of its work into one processor, which combines the work and produces output.

Originally, the Japanese were expected to accept dataflow technology in their working plan for the fifth-generation. But that idea was tentatively discarded. They claim that they will take advantage of dataflow technology, but the final product will be something other than dataflow. Their goal is to produce machines with a million or more small processors. The result will be, according to Dr. Kashiro Fuchi, head of ICOT, between one thousand and ten thousand megaflops for general use.

Computer capacity can also be measured by the speed at which a system handles logical steps. This is especially important in AI, because the most intuitive and seemingly automatic human intellectual processes often require the largest number of programming steps in machines. For example, making one inference in a natural-language program requires between one hundred and one thousand steps. The most powerful computers can perform about ten thousand logical steps a second. According to Fuchi, the Japanese target is between one hundred thousand and one million logical steps a second.

The first fifth-generation machine is expected to be ready as a prototype in 1985. It will be a personal computer. This machine will lack parallel processors, but it will contain a very large amount of memory, and it will be the basis of the generation of machines with giant capacities. The total internal memory of this machine is expected to be about eighty megabytes. Fuchi claims that this machine will be considered crude by the end of the ten-year period. By that time, he believes, the Japanese will have developed a machine called the Parallel Inferential Machine, which will have an internal memory of at least one hundred billion bytes.

A project of this size will obviously involve many new technologies and inventions. Some will come from projects already underway. For example, the Super Speed Computing Project, also under MITI jurisdiction, has been working on powerful microchips. Its main thrust is to discover ways of placing more transistors on each chip. Present technology allows up to about three hundred transistors. The goal of the project is to increase that capacity to ten million.

Natural-language systems will be incorporated in every fifth-generation machine. But the plan is to go further and program computers to accept oral input and produce oral output. As pointed out in Chapter 3, voice-recognition systems that work with many different users are not within current technical capability. Current technology in such systems is inadequate for any practical use. These systems normally can be used by only one or two speakers. Users must speak very slowly, and the vocabularies of the systems are extremely limited. Even with these restrictions, current machines often make errors. According to officials, the Japanese machines must be "user-tuned" a bit. Each machine will be able to be used by a few hundred speakers. The Japanese expect that, by the end of the ten-year period, their prototype machines will be able to accept continuous human speech and will contain vocabularies of fifty thousand words. Accuracy will be about ninety-five percent. The machines will be able to carry on question-and-answer conversations with humans. Voice-operated typewriters will also be provided.

Building such voice-recognition systems and other systems that are far beyond current technological capability in a ten-year period will require an almost superhuman effort of intellect. The Japanese understand this and plan to make extensive use of AI machines in their research. For example, as the number of papers becomes too numerous for humans to handle, machines will be ready to read and digest the material. As seen in the chapter on natural-language systems (Chapter 3), such machines already exist in a crude form. But the Japanese expect their machines to be truly useful in that they will extract material relevant to a specific user. In other words, a scientist may be able to tell a computer of his or her research interests, and the computer will not only choose the papers that match his interests but will also extract the relevant sections of those papers.

PROJECT PROSPECTS

Will this very ambitious project work? It is impossible for us to know. Fifth-generation machines will depend on technologies that have never been proved workable; and, if the technological breakthroughs on which the Japanese are counting do not come about on schedule, the whole project will have to be extended or possibly even abandoned.

But, in the world of computers, ten years is a long time. In the days of ENIAC, the current crop of tiny, powerful computers was probably not even a dream. In any ten-year period from 1945 to the present, says one researcher, computers have become more powerful by a factor of about fifty.

What may disturb us then is not that the Japanese are dreaming of what may happen ten years from now, but rather that they are planning it with too much specificity. There is no doubt, however, that the goal is honorable. And even if only twenty percent of it is reached in ten years (or eighty percent in twenty years), humankind will have made a great technological advance. And, if nothing else, the Japanese plan provides a prototype agenda that AI researchers can use as a guide.

■ THREE ■

PROGRAMMING AI

• 11 •

Programming Intelligence

All modern computers—whether they happen to be for AI or for "normal" applications—work in the same way: They are only capable of sensing whether their circuits are on or off. This simple function holds true when a computer adds two and two and when it infers a nuance in a language. Therefore, AI programming is similar in many ways to the programming used for any business or scientific application.

For example, take the algebraic problem, $A - B = C$. This also happens to be a BASIC programming language expression. When the computer with BASIC is given this information, it is able to make certain assumptions about the relationships among A, B, and C. For example, it knows that $A - C = B$ and $A - (B + C) = 0$. The computer is able to make these assumptions because BASIC and other computer languages include general rules about equations. It is possible to represent truths about propositions or to represent statements about the real world in a similar manner. And it is also possible to program these truths into a computer. Although the actual method of programming AI applications is beyond the scope of this book, discussing how knowledge is represented symbolically is valuable here.

REPRESENTATION OF KNOWLEDGE

Knowledge can be represented symbolically through the use of a very basic method called *propositional logic*. A proposition is any statement that can be either true or false. Examples include "All the boys in class are here" and "Count Dracula lives." Propositional logic is a means of determining the truth or falsity of a statement by referring both to knowledge previously received and to the rules for manipulating that knowledge.

We do this automatically as we think. For example, we might refute the proposition, "Dracula lives," by reasoning that:

1. Human vampires do not exist.
2. Count Dracula is a human vampire.
3. Count Dracula does not exist.

But propositional logic is valuable in programming because it does not need specific words; it works with letters in a way that is similar to the way algebra works with letters. For example, the proposition, "Human vampires exist," could be represented by the letter "q." A proposition that is false is represented by a letter preceded by the word "not." "Human vampires do not exist" could be represented by "not q." The truth or falsity of a single proposition cannot be determined by itself. Other facts, other propositions that we know are either true or false, are necessary before we can made any judgments. This also happens in algebra, in which we cannot know that $Y = 3$ without first knowing that $X = Y + Z$, $X = 5$, and $Z = 2$.

In math, we represent relationships among numbers by using arithmetic signs ($-, +, \times$, and so forth). In logic, we use connectives ("not," "or," "and," and "implies").

The simplest connective to use is "not." We know that something is either true or not true. Consider the proposition, "Frank is a living human being who is a boy."

Either it is true or it is false. It cannot be both true and false, and it cannot be neither true nor false. Let us call this proposition "p." In general, we can say the following about propositions and the "not" connective:

1. If p is true, then not p is false.
2. If p is false, then not p is true.
3. If not p is true, then p is false.
4. If not p is false, then p is true.

This can be simply represented in a *truth table*. The left side of the table represents p, the right side, not p. F represents false, and T represents true. In the first row, we see that if p is true, then not p is false; in the second row, we see that if p is true, then not p is false; in the second row, we see that if p is false, then not p is true.

P	NOT P
T	F
F	T

Slightly more complicated is the truth table using the connective. We know that if one or both of two statements connected in one proposition by "or" are true, then the proposition is true. "I have a ball or I have a bat" is an example.

Either "I have a ball" or "I have a bat" is true or both statements are true. "Or" in propositional logic is different from "or" in customary English usage in that it is not used in the exclusive sense; that is, I can have a ball *and* a bat, and the above proposition would be true. In other words, the proposition is true if either *or both* of the following are true:

1. I have a ball.
2. I have a bat.

The only way that the proposition can be false is if both 1 and 2 are false. This is how the truth table for the "or" connective looks:

P Q	P OR Q
T T	T
T F	T
F T	T
F F	F

"I have a ball *and* I have a bat" is true only if both 1 and 2 are true. Here is the table for the "and" connective:

P Q	P AND Q
T T	T
T F	F
F T	F
F F	F

The "implies" connective is the same as the if/then combination in many programming languages. "If it snows, then I will shovel the drive" is the same as " 'If it snows' implies 'I will shovel the drive' " is the same as " 'p' implies 'q'."

The only way this proposition can be wrong is if p is true and q is false (i.e., it is snowing, and I am not going to shovel the drive).

In any other combination, the proposition is correct. If p is false (it is not snowing), and if q is true (I am going to shovel the drive), or if q is false (I am not going to shovel the drive), the proposition is correct. Here is the "implies" table:

P Q	P IMPLIES Q
T T	T
T F	F
F T	T
F F	T

This table shows that a false proposition implies any proposition. For example, "If you can fly implies I am a monkey's uncle" and "If Count Dracula is here implies I am a vampire too" are true.

PREDICATE LOGIC

A slightly more complicated, but more compact way of exploring logical truths is called *predicate logic*. With this method, items that are discussed in the proposition are taken out of the sentence and are separated from the phrase that explains the relationship between them. In "The ball is in the glove," the two items are "ball" and "glove," and the words "is in" explain the relationship.

The correct form uses one word to explain the relationship (IN) and one word to represent each object (BALL, GLOVE). The word that represents the relationship is called the *predicate*, the items to which the predicate refers are called the *arguments*.

The proper form of expressing the proposition is:

PREDICATE (ARGUMENTS)
or
IN (BALL,GLOVE)

We can use any table to determine the truth or falsity of any proposition written in this form. For example, "If her car is in the drive, she will be home" can be represented as IN(CAR,DRIVE) implies AT(SHE,HOME), which is the same as "p implies q" and which can be worked out using the "implies" table.

A common way of representing the results of a logical argument is as follows:

1. IN(CAR,DRIVE)
2. IN(CAR,DRIVE) implies AT(SHE,HOME)
3. AT(SHE,HOME)

The given part of the argument is steps 1 and 2, and the logical conclusion is step 3.

By the way, it is important to note that the following argument is not correct because of line 3 of the "implies" table.

1. not (CAR,DRIVE)
2. IN(CAR,DRIVE) implies AT(SHE,HOME)
3. not AT(SHE,HOME)

Programming Predicate Logic

So far, we have used predicate logic to represent very specific pieces of information. Of course, a computer that is programmed with world knowledge cannot have such specific instructions about the world. What is necessary is to generalize the world sufficiently so that the data base won't become unwieldy or impossible. The way to accomplish this is to use variables.

For example, it is obvious to humans that if a person is in a car, then that person will be wherever that car is. But it is certainly not obvious to the on and off circuits of a computer, unless this information is entered. Here is a representation of that truth:

AT(CAR,x) and IN(y,CAR) implies AT(x,y)

The location of the car is represented by x. Anything (a person, animal, or thing) that is in the car is represented by y. So, if the car is at place (x), any person, animal, or thing (y) that is in the car will also be at that place.

The proposition can be made even more general:

AT(x,y) and IN(z,x) implies AT(z,y)

Or, anything that is in something will be located wherever that something is located. Put another way: if x is at y, and z is in x, then z is at y.

Here are some more variables:

MAN(x) implies not FLY(x)

This means that if a thing is a man (x), it cannot fly.

BIRD(x) implies FLY(x)

This means that if a thing is a bird, it can fly. But, in reality, these sentences have to be qualified further to account for airplanes and non-flying birds.

Most knowledge-based systems use predicate logic. In Chapter 5, for example, we discussed a technique that the system uses to discover what it is looking at by playing Twenty Questions. (e.g., Can the object fly? Can it swim? and so on). The program knowledge that allows the computer to make use of the answers to these questions must be represented in the forms above.

In those forms, the letter "x" is called an *individual constant*. That is, it represents a specific man or a specific bird. In logic, the existence of something is asserted by naming the thing with a letter.

Often, the existence of something depends on the existence of other things. For example, a person cannot be an employer unless he or she has employees. A person cannot be a father unless the person is male and has children. And there can be no painter without paintings.

We represent these contingent beings by functions. An employer is a function of an employee. A father is a function of a child. And a painter is a function of a painting.

So, if we state the existence of the individual constant EMPLOYEE(x), we know that there is some function of x that we represent as $f(x)$, which is the employer. Here are three examples:

1. EMPLOYEE(x) implies EMPLOYER $(f(x),x)$
2. PAINTING(x) implies PAINTER $(f(x),x)$
3. CHILD(x) implies FATHER $(f(x),x)$

In the first example, we are stating that there is an employee x. We then assert that there must be an employer, which is a function of x and which we call $f(x)$. The last part of the proposition is that $f(x)$ is the employer of x.

Representing functions is very useful in representing knowledge. Without understanding the relationship between things, the computer would be aware only of the existence of isolated, individual objects. Representing what each object can do would be difficult, if not impossible. And representing things such as motivation, physical proximity, and other relationships *would* be impossible.

In computation, logical arguments are found to be true or false through the *resolution method*, which is used on propositions such as the following:

1. x or y or z
2. (not x) or a or b
3. y or z or a or b

If the two top arguments are correct, then the third argument is true. Very simply, we can say that x and not x cancel each other out.

Each part of the proposition that is complete (that cannot be broken down) is called an *atom*. In other words, a predicate and its arguments make up one atom. HAVE(I,BALL) is an atom. A *literal* is an atom with or without "not" in front of it. Both HAVE(I,BALL) and not (HAVE(I,BALL)) are literals; the first is a *positive literal*, the second is a *negative literal*.

Now that we know the terminology, we can go back to the literals resolved above. A more general way of making that resolution is:

1. x or y
2. not (x)
3. y

We have discovered the one true literal. Plugging in the values for x and y with a real-world situation, we can get:

1. AT(JOHN,HOME) or AT(JOHN,WORK)
2. not (AT(JOHN, HOME))
3. AT(JOHN,WORK)

In the first proposition, the first literal states that John is at home, and the second states that John is at work. The "or" connective tells us that at least one of the atoms is true.

There are many other rules for manipulating propositions. Here are some examples:

1. not (not p) = p The negative of a negative equals a positive.
2. (not p) or q = p implies q. One of the two propositions (either not p or q) has to be correct, the other incorrect. If not p is incorrect, then q is correct. P means not p is incorrect, so q must be correct.
3. not (p and q) = (not p) or (not q)
4. not (p or q) = (not p) and (not q)
5. (p and q) or r = (p or r) and (q or r)

With these and other rules, a computer performs calculations on logical functions.

PROGRAMMING LOGIC

LISP

The most common programming language used in AI programs is LISP. John McCarthy invented LISP as a language that could manipulate not only numbers but also logical concepts.

Data is entered into LISP through what is called an *S-expression*, which may be an atom or a dotted pair. An atom in LISP is similar to an atom in logic. It is the smallest expression that exists. That is, it is an expression that cannot be broken down into smaller expressions without destroying it. An atom is written in most LISP dialects as a string of characters beginning with a letter (unless it is a numeric atom, which contains only numbers). HOUSE, XYZ, and BLACKPEN, may all be atoms. Most LISP dialects allow for atoms of any size, up to one line.

Atoms can be joined in dotted pairs. This is accomplished by surrounding them with parentheses and by separating them with a period. For example, (HELLO.MOTHER) is a dotten pair made up of the atoms HELLO and MOTHER. Joining atoms is called *CONSing*; the result is a *CONS*. In other words, by CONSing the atoms HELLO and MOTHER, we arrive at the dotted pair (HELLO.MOTHER). And (HELLO.MOTHER) is the CONS of the atoms HELLO and MOTHER.

We also see that dotted pairs can also be CONSed, as in (HELLO.MOTHER).(HELLO.FATHER). And atoms can be joined with dotted pairs, as in HELLO.(MOTHER.FATHER). Everything to the left of the first period represents the main CONS. Dotted pairs can be made to be as long as you wish.

The dotted pair can be divided into two parts. The first part begins with the letter that is leftmost and continues until the main period. This part is called the CAR.

The information from the CAR to the rightmost parenthesis (in other words, everything after the CAR) is called the CDR. A complex dotted pair can consist of many CARs and CDRs if the pair were broken down, but at any one time, there can be only one CAR and one CDR.

(HUSBAND.WIFE).(WALK.QUICKLY).(STORE)

LISTP and ATOM are two "recognizers." Their function is to determine if an expression is an atom or a dotted pair. If an expression is a LISTP, it is not an ATOM, and vice versa.

Here are some definitions that can be computed:

LISTP/CONS(x,y) The CONS of x and y is a LISTP (dotted pair).
CAR(CONS(x,y)) = x The CAR of CONSing x and y = x.
CDR(CONS(x,y)) = y The CDR or the CONS of x.y is y.

An alternative means of representing expressions in LISP is through LIST. The form of LIST is similar to that of predicate logic. Most dialects of LISP allow for the elimination of periods and the substitution of commas and parentheses to follow predicate logic notation. Here are some predicate logic expressions and LISP counterparts:

AT(MARY,HOME)   (AT MARY HOME)
PERSON(x)   (PERSON x)

In LISP, the function comes first. So, 5 plus 5 or $5+5$ is represented in LISP as (PLUS 5 5). Multiplication is represented in a similar manner (TIMES 3 5), as is division (QUOTIENT 10 2), square root (SQRT 9), and so on.

CDR,CAR, and CONS can be used as functions. CDR, for example, will find a list's CDR (everything after the CAR); so, CDR(JOHN MARY JACK) produces MARY JACK. CAR finds the first element; CAR(JOHN MARY JACK) produces JOHN. And CONS joins members to a list; CONS JOHN (MARY JACK) produces (JOHN MARY JACK).

Variables are assigned in LISP using SETQ (similar to the LET expression in BASIC).

(SETQ X 5) assigns the value 5 to X.

A typical LISP program is a number of functions that are defined by the user. An example is:

DEFINE(SQUARE X)(TIMES X X) We have defined a function
SQUARE to be a number times itself.

Expressions in LISP can be tested for truth (T) or falsity (N for NIL). (EQUAL x x) produces T, (EQUAL x y) produces N, (LESSP 3 5) produces T, and (LESSP 5 3) produces N.

ACT I

A newer programming language being developed for use in AI programs is called ACT I. The philosophy on which ACT I has been developed is that it is more important to incorporate the knowledge of a society, rather than the knowledge of only one expert, into a system. Therefore, ACT I works as if many different individuals were involved in solving a problem—with each individual contributing information.

To solve problems, each part of the program must be able to communicate with each other part. This is done with *message passing,* which is the basis of ACT I.

Each part of the program must work in parallel to each other part so that speed can be maintained. Avoiding timing errors while doing this necessitates careful programming. ACT I provides means to facilitate integration of tasks.

The only type of data in ACT I is the *ab actor*, which can be a procedure or a piece of data. Actors are differentiated by how they behave when they receive messages. Each actor reasons differently. When a message is passed to an actor, its program (or *script*) views the message and determines if it can accept it. This is a function of whether the script has any procedures for dealing with the content of the message.

Each actor's script has procedures in it for sending a message to delegate responsibility to another actor for the script. The receiving actor might be more expert in solving the problem at hand, it might have more general knowledge about the problem, or it might be better equipped to know the best actor to which to relay the message.

As information is assigned to an actor, that information (including procedures) becomes part of its script. If we assign, for example, the name JOHN to variable k, this information is given to an actor specializing in variables. When any other actor receives a message containing the variable k, it then knows to which actor the message must be sent.

One advantage of ACT I over LISP is in the introduction of new types of data. LISP requires that the user introduce data by using data objects defined by the language developers. Being able to define new types of data makes ACT I more suitable for developing new procedures.

As the language consists of small modules, each performing a small part of what might be a complete procedure, it becomes extremely easy to modify and extend a program. This is done simply by defining new actors rather than by rewriting entire procedures. An actor is defined when it is named and when it is identified by its acquaintances, which are other actors that may need to work with it.

Probably the most important advantage of ACT I is in its presently theoretical ability to perform parallel processing, in which many different processors work on one problem at the same time. Because each actor is a self-sufficient unit that contains all information necessary to perform one specific task, many bottlenecking problems that result when parallel processors attempt to gain access to centralized information are eliminated. In one model for parallel processing, the actors would be distributed through many different processors, which may be remotely located from one another. Because all communication is performed by message passing, and because actors, not users, determine which message goes where, the operator would not have to know if the actor being addressed is in a nearby processor or in a processor thousands of miles away.

· 12 ·

Problem Solving

Almost all AI programs contain problem-solving strategies. The first true AI programs were probably developed to solve general problems. One of these programs, the General Problem Solver (GPS), is discussed in Chapter 14.

Many problems can be broken down into three elements: an initial state, a goal state, and an operator. As the problem-solving process develops, there is also a constantly changing current state.

THE TOWER OF HANOI

Let's look at these states in the context of an actual problem. One of the first problems successfully solved by an AI program is the Tower of Hanoi problem.

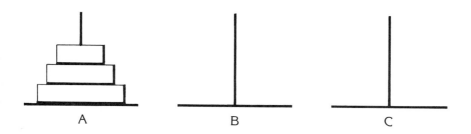

A   B   C

This puzzle has three pegs labeled A, B, and C. Three disks of different sizes are on peg A. The disks are arranged from largest to smallest, with the smallest being on top. The preceding figure represents the initial state.

The goal is to transfer the disks to peg C, while arranging them in the same descending order of size found in the initial state. The next figure represents the goal state.

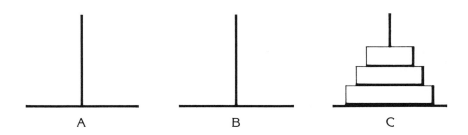

A   B   C

The operator is the action of moving the disks using the following rules:

1. Only one disk can be moved at a time.
2. Each time a disk is moved, it must be placed on a peg.
3. At no time can a larger disk be placed on top of a smaller disk.

The procedure is to move a disk so as to (1) bring the current state closer to the goal state, or (2) make any legal move if goal 1 is not possible.

The following figure depicts the steps to the solution. Although solving this problem is not difficult, seeing how the steps follow the procedure can be informative.

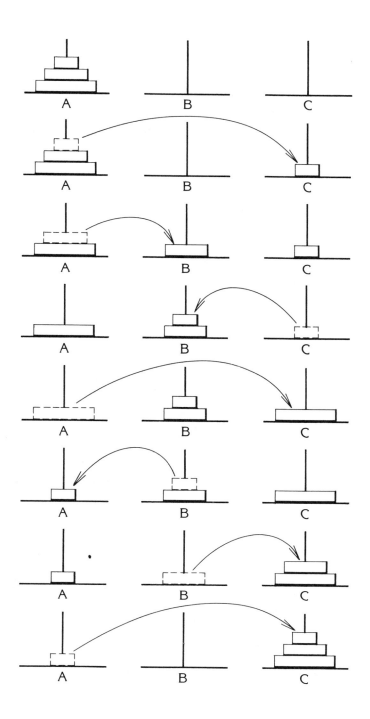

Steps 1, 2, and 3 bring the current situation closer to the goal. Steps 4 and 6 bring the current situation closer to the initial situation. Notice that in step 6 we could have placed the smallest disk on C, because that would have been a legal move and it would have fulfilled the objective of moving closer to the final state. That action, however, only adds unnecessary steps to attaining the final goal.

Machines usually solve "state" problems by generating a state graph. The next figure is a state graph of the Tower of Hanoi problem.

Each circle (or *node*) represents one current state. The lines coming from and going toward the nodes are called *arcs*. Each node in the graph

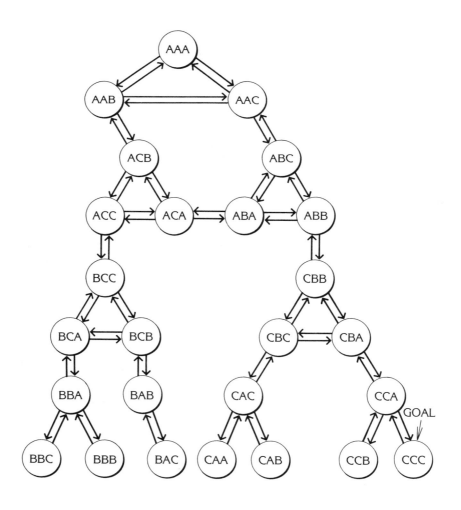

has three letters. The first letter represents the peg on which the largest disk rests, the second letter represents the peg on which the middle-size disk rests, and the third letter represents the peg on which the smallest disk rests.

The initial node has all three disks on peg A. The final or goal node has all three disks on peg C. The most direct solution to this problem can be found by following the graph through the route that leads to this goal node.

Of course, few problems are as simple to solve as our three-disk version of the Tower of Hanoi game. The original game used 64 disks and required 30×10^{30} nodes. Generating a graph for this version is an almost impossible task for human or machine. One solution is to generate the graph node by node. A complete path is generated until it either reaches the goal or hits a dead end. If it hits a dead end, the next path is generated, and so on. This is called an *implicit graph*.

In the Tower of Hanoi problem, the path from the initial state to the goal state on the state graph is clear. Even generating an implicit graph is not difficult, because very few nodes must be examined. In more complex problems, however, including a search strategy in the program becomes necessary. The purpose of a search strategy is to eliminate the chance of going on wild goose chases that lead after many hours of computing time to dead ends.

SEARCHING WITH STATE GRAPHS

To understand search strategies, we have to look a bit more closely at state graphs. In AI terminology, a state graph is often called a *state space* or a *tree*. A tree begins with one root (drawn at the top, as on a family tree). This root gives birth to one or more children, which represent the different nodes of the problem. Each child (or offspring) may give birth to other children, in which case the original child becomes a parent while remaining a child to its own parent. Arcs go from node to node in a graph and are usually called branches. Branches are often not equipped with arrows, because movement is always from the root downward. Each parent can have many children, but each child can have only one parent. Children of the same node are called twins. A childless node (in other words, a dead-end or a goal node) is called a leaf. Successive levels of offspring are called depths, which are numbered from zero—the root—up. Children of the root are at depth 1, their children are at depth 2, and so on. Sometimes a part of a tree must break off. When this happens, the broken part then becomes a subtree—with its own root, branches, children, leaves, and so on. Here is an example of a tree:

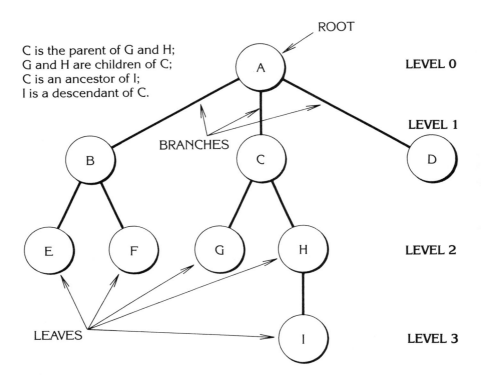

C is the parent of G and H;
G and H are children of C;
C is an ancestor of I;
I is a descendant of C.

ROOT

LEVEL 0

LEVEL 1

BRANCHES

LEVEL 2

LEAVES

LEVEL 3

As mentioned, most problems do not permit the entire tree (or graph) to be generated at one time; hence, different search strategies have been developed.

Breadth-First Search

A breadth-first search expands a tree level by level. First, all root children are generated. If the goal node is not found among these, then level 2 is generated, and so on. The following is an example of a breadth-first search.

The advantage of using a breadth-first search is that finding the shortest path from the root to the goal node is assured. Because each

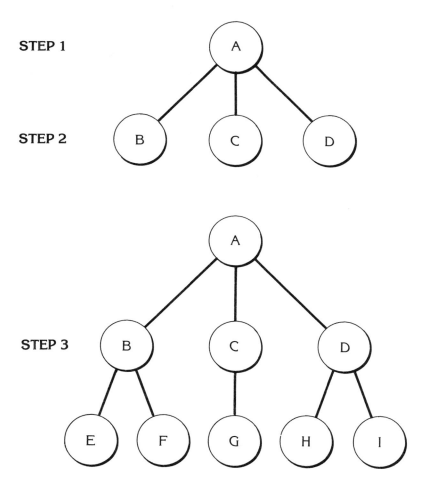

STEP 1

STEP 2

STEP 3

level is explored before a new level is generated, inadvertently taking a "longcut" (by following a path down below the goal node) is not possible. Breadth-first searches, however, present a disadvantage in that redundant operations are required. In a program, movement from node to node involves performing some operation on the parent node. To return from the child node to the parent node, that operation must be repeated. In the figure, generating the children of node B requires that the computer perform an operation leading to node E. The computer then must repeat that operation to return to B. It performs the operation once again to get to E, and so on.

Depth-First Search

A depth-first search expands the tree along one path until it reaches a goal, a dead end, or a path already traveled. The following figure depicts a depth-first search.

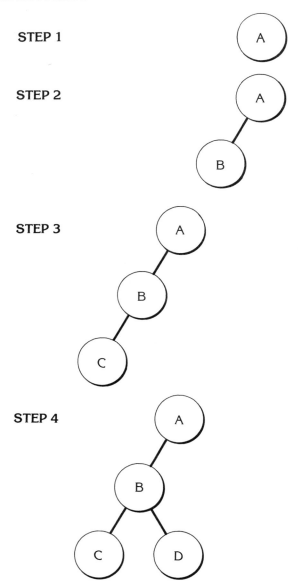

The obvious advantage of such a search is that it eliminates the need for constant backtracking. However, a number of disadvantages exist: First, the path used to reach the goal might not be the quickest path; second, such a search might increase rather than decrease the number of calculations needed to find the goal; and third, a root might lead to an infinite number of children or at least to such a large number as to keep the computer working for years. (The solution to this last problem is to place a restriction on the number of levels the computer should search before returning to the root and trying again. This solution, however, introduces the possibility of never reaching the goal. If a goal is at level 10, and the maximum search depth (also called the depth bound) is set at level 9, then the solution will not be found.)

Programmers study problems carefully to determine the most advantageous depth bound. The depth bound must be deep enough to ensure that a solution will be found. But it must also be shallow enough to avoid too much unnecessary computation.

Although breadth-first and depth-first searches can produce satisfactory results with some problems, their failings are easy to see. The computer is forced to travel blindly along every path and to stop at predetermined depths or breadths before moving on—perhaps missing the goal that was one depth below. The success of the computer depends on its brute force in juggling thousands of routes at very high speed. And, while using great speed rather than intelligence is a legitimate problem-solving technique, many problems cannot be solved in this way using even the most powerful computers. Programs must be made to approximate human intelligence in problem solving. Humans do not blindly examine all possible solutions, but rather they use rules of thumb by which they estimate which routes are likely to yield the correct solution. These rules of thumb, heuristics, are discussed briefly in Chapter 2.

SEARCHING WITH HEURISTICS

When a program uses heuristics to guide a search, it executes an ordered search rather than a blind search. A blind search is characterized either by a complete breadth-first or depth-first search or at best by predetermined rules governing the search. The rules governing an ordered search are generated during the search. (Information gained from the search itself produces rules that govern further searching.)

In general, the purpose of a heuristic search is to find the most economical path from the initial state to the goal state. The total number of operations the computer must perform—the number of arcs on a state graph—represents the cost of the search. The object of a heuristic program is to find the route with the fewest arcs.

To find the route with the fewest arcs, two calculations or estimates must be made. The first is a determination of the cost (the number of arcs) from the initial state to the present state. In many problems, this can be done with certainty; in other problems, more than one route connects the initial state to the present state, and the cost of some of these routes is not always the number of arcs traveled. In other words, the cost of the shortest route should be considered.Therefore, backtracking up the tree to determine the true cost of the path to the present position is sometimes necessary.

The second calculation is the cost of the path from the present position to the final or goal node. This estimate must be made using heuristics that are unique to the problem.

Using heuristics, a program may make a preliminary determination that a particular route will cost 8 levels. All other routes are expected to cost 10 levels, so the 8-level route is chosen. Let A equal the total cost of the search (8, in this case). Let B equal the cost from the root node to the present node (say, 3). And let C equal the cost from the present node to the final node (by computation, 5). Note that A is estimated, B is known, and C is determined by subtracting B from A. As the tree is expanded, the program discovers that C does not actually drop to 4 after the next node is reached; C remains at 5. Thus, the total cost of the route will have to be at least 9. The program can continue on this route because 9 is still lower than any of the other routes. The next expansion again gives a value of 5 for C, making A a minimium of 10. Once again, the program can continue on the route, this time because all other routes have estimated values of at least 10. But if the program goes one step further without lowering the value of C, then this route is no longer viewed as the most economical, and the program will backtrack and try the next most likely route.

The above method of heuristic search limits the depth of the search, but there are many other methods of using heuristics. For example, heuristics can be used to choose which children the program should completely disregard. Other heuristics might point out certain promising nodes that should be expanded despite their estimated high costs.

Heuristic searches will be discussed further in Chapter 13.

SEARCHING WITH SUBGOALS

In many real-world problems, the state graph method, as described, is not satisfactory. First, the number of paths might be too large. If so, even if the computer is using a heuristic, simply applying a heuristic to each of the nodes would take up more computational time than is practical. Second, many problems are too large to work with. One solution is to break down a problem into subroutines or subgoals. A subgoal is simply one step on the road from the initial position to the goal.

Humans regularly use subgoals in solving problems. If we are planning a trip, for example, we first decide on the mode of transportation and buy a plane ticket or rent a car or make sure our own car has fuel. Then we might choose a motel located along our route. We would drive to that motel. And so on.

Humans solve other problems by treating them as wholes. When using a highway map to choose a route, most people prefer to view the map as a whole. However, programming a computer to view the map as a whole and to apply a heuristic to each possible route is difficult. This type of programming is made much easier through the use of subgoals. For many problems that contain so many possible alternatives—we will discuss some of these problems in Chapter 13—generating and solving subgoals become a necessity.

Subgoals with Single Operators

In developing subgoals, the computer must first generate the subgoal out of the larger goal and must then plan the sequence of subgoals. One method of doing this is by programming into the computer an operator that, when applied, produces a subgoal. In our cross-country trip, the key operator might be to find a straight route that, when traveled, results in the new difference between the goal state and the present state being less than the current difference between those two states. By applying this operator, a continuous succession of subgoals would be generated until the goal state is reached.

This method of subgoal planning, of determining and then lessening the difference between the present and goal states, is one of the earliest to be used in AI programming. It has worked well on mazes and on very simple logic problems.

This procedure will work only when the path from the present state to the goal state is spanned by a number of short, mostly repetitive actions. Sometimes this condition does not exist. Suppose we want to design an invention in which there are so many parts that it consists of a jumble of different goals. An architect designing a house, for example, cannot simply apply a single operator or even a number of operators over and over. Another problem arises from the way the lessening of physical distance is used as a measure of the closeness to the goal. In some problems, many tasks might reduce the difference between the current state and the goal state, but they do this in such a trivial way as to be inefficient. A common joke in this regard concerns the goal of traveling from the earth to the moon—the first subgoal produced by the computer is: Climb a tree.

Another problem with subgoal planning is that in many situations the difference between two states does not yield any hint as to the best way to lessen that difference. With both the architect and the moon traveler, there is no way of looking just at the initial state (i.e., at the building lot or at the astronaut on earth) and the goal state (i.e., the completed building and the astronaut on the moon) to understand any of the necessary actions that would bring about the goal state.

And, finally, this method does not allow for the interaction of various operators. Most real-life situations are constantly changing, and any action may affect the current situation in such a way that finding a new operator may be necessary. Traveling from Maine to California will work using the difference-reduction method only if the car doesn't break down (and has to be towed 20 miles backward rather than 100 miles forward to the nearest service station).

Subgoals with Two or More Operators

A slightly more complicated method of generating subgoals is to use a number of operators rather than just one. When a given condition exists, the correct operator is applied. Sometimes a search tree is set up just to discover the correct operator that must be used.

Problem solving through subgoals can be broken down into two general categories. In "AND" solving, a final solution is not found until all subgoals have been achieved. We cannot drive from Maine to California without achieving all subgoals, which are made up of short routes along the way.

You will recall a state graph "expands" when it generates another node. When a problem-reduction state graph is generated using the AND method, the state graph is called an AND expansion.

The other way to generate subgoals is by using the "OR" method, in which completion of any one subgoal will result in the achievement of the final goal. There may be many routes that go across town, for example. Each would be a subgoal in the OR expansion, because taking any one of them would lead to achieving the goal of getting across town. A state graph representation of OR expansion would resemble the state graph representations described earlier (the Tower of Hanoi, for example).

Most state graphs are not entirely AND or OR, but rather "AND/OR." Usually, a number of subgoals must be achieved, as in an

AND expansion. And other subgoals are alternatives, as in an OR expansion.

In all the examples given thus far, the human programmer is very closely involved in the solving of the problem. Operators come from preprogrammed input, as does the definition of the goals and sometimes even of the subgoals. Unfortunately, preprogramming input is not always possible in the writing of programs that function in the unpredictable, real world. A specific plan or set of operators cannot be prescribed for responding to an infinite number of problems. The program must have a way of discovering—on its own—tactics and strategies for solving a problem.

One way to do this is to have the program follow a hierarchy of plans. The first plan generates a general strategy for attacking a problem. The next plan refines that strategy and generates alternatives to be followed when certain obstacles or problems arise. At each step of the way, the plan is further refined.

If we wanted to build a house, for example, we would not first study in detail how to dig a foundation, dig it, and then study how to position the supporting beams, and so forth. Following this procedure might cause later problems, because performing a step in a later subgoal might be made more difficult by its being performed later and not earlier. Therefore, the intelligent carpenter would first learn in general terms how to build a house. He or she would learn the different tasks, such as digging the foundation, framing, sheetrocking, installing the plumbing, and so on. Next, the carpenter would learn how each operation relates to the others. This would provide a general overview of the order in which operations should be performed. And finally, the carpenter would learn the specifics of each operation—that is, how to sheetrock or to frame.

This example is, of course, much too simple, because each operation consists of many subgoals in itself. For our purposes, however, the example is a valuable study of how a program with a hierarchical structure might function in the planning of the building of a house.

This program would be built with the roughest and most general plan—the overall understanding of how a house is built—on top. Next, subgoals related to the interaction of the various projects would be programmed. And finally, all subgoals related to the processes of each operation would be programmed.

The first task of the program might be to generate a list of materials. To do this, it would only need to work in the first level of goals, in understanding how a house is built. Also at this level, the computer can generate a list of which contractors to call. But scheduling the contractors forces the computer to descend to the second level, which determines the interaction of the projects. This level ensures that the sheetrock will not be applied before the insulation is installed. If a contractor gets sick and cannot complete a job, the third level, which has information about individual jobs, would be consulted to determine what has yet to be completed. The program then backs up to the first level to see what other jobs can be done while a new carpenter is sought.

The advantage of hierarchical programming is that heuristics can be used on every level. This is possible because each level is able to get information from every other level. For example, if the program is to use the problem-reduction method to solve the problem of the sick carpenter, the complete state graph of the project must be searched. This task is much too large to be practical. But, if each level consisted of isolated subgoals, the program would halt dead in its tracks when confronted with a sick contractor. Hierarchical programming allows the project to be broken down into reasonable chunks without isolating any one part of it.

Another example of how this hierarchy of goals can be used is in the programming of robots. The highest level would be the instructions to the robot. One instruction might be "PLACE A SCREW IN HOLE AND TIGHTEN IT." The second level would contain specific instructions for each task (such as removing a screw from a hopper, lining up holes, placing the screw in the holes, and so forth). The third level might be obstacle-avoidance routines. The robot begins with the first level. In carrying out the instruction at this level, it immediately hits on the problem of attaining a screw. To obtain a screw, the robot goes to the second level. Once the screw is in hand, the robot returns to the first level to find out what to do with the screw. If there is an object in front of the part to be screwed, the robot goes to the third level.

Although all AI programs, from natural-language to image-understanding systems, use some of the techniques discussed in this chapter, the specifics of such complex applications are far beyond the scope of this book. The next chapter provides an understanding of programming procedures in a slightly complex application—game playing.

· 13 ·

Game Playing

Looking at programs that play games is a good way to observe AI techniques in action. These programs encompass many of the problems and successes of the field as a whole.

Viewed one way, a game—a game of skill—is the purest example of intelligent decision-making behavior. Most techniques involved in programming games are the same as those used in other areas of intelligent decision making. As you read this chapter, you will quickly notice that the techniques are the same as or are similar to those discussed in the previous chapter. For example, an initial state and a goal state exist in every game. A state graph or tree is generated; the initial state is represented by the root, and each position is represented by a node. Each move in a game results in the generation of other nodes—new game positions. The goal of each player is to reach the final position—the winning position—before the opponent does.

The difference between games and real-world programming is that games can be controlled more. The number of different possible game positions in a chess game, for example, is smaller than the number of possible contingencies in the real world. Because a game provides a limited number of possible responses, its program can be much more simple than a real-world program.

However, games like chess and checkers have so many possible variations that searching a complete tree is as impossible as it is with real-world programs. And games approach real-world situations much more than puzzles do, because games are not under anyone's complete control (at least two players' wills are involved).

Game trees, which are similar to state graphs, are used to represent games. For every position, two game trees can be generated, one for the player and one for the opponent. In a game tree, the root represents the original position of the pieces. The branches or arcs represent the various legal moves. And each child represents the game position after a move is made.

Game trees are AND/OR search trees. When a player moves, he or she only has to make one of the many moves that lead to a leaf in his or her favor—a win. When the opponent moves, the original player has no choices and can make no moves; the opponent has to make all the moves that lead to the first player's loss.

HEURISTICS IN GAME PLAYING

The most exacting way to play a game would be to generate a complete game tree. This tree would present all possible board positions and would show graphically the route to the winning position. The result would be a perfect game. Unfortunately, the large number of possible game positions makes this impossible for most games. There are an estimated 10^{20} possible moves in the average chess position. The most powerful computers would not be able to generate a complete game tree in any reasonable amount of time. In fact, state-of-the-art technology would take from now until the sun burned out to generate a complete chess game tree. Therefore, programs must depend on heuristic methods to shorten the search. The object of a search is a node that leads to a win. And each node must have some means of labeling its probabilities of leading to a win, a loss, or a draw. In most cases, especially in the early moves of the game, most nodes may lead to all three outcomes, depending on further play (by both players, in a chess game). In this case, the node is given the most optimistic label. In other words, a node that may lead to either a win or a draw will be labeled a win. Obviously, the game tree for one player would be the opposite of the other's. A loss for one would mean a win for the other. But at the beginning, most nodes could lead to wins, so each player's tree would have many win nodes.

If a computer could generate a complete tree, its course of action would be simple: move through the nodes that lead to the quickest route to a win leaf. But, as we have seen, generating this tree is impossible for most games. The procedure for finding the best moves must be more economical. To find such a procedure, AI researchers have studied the way human experts play games.

In a game of chess, for example, even a grandmaster cannot look more than five or six moves ahead in most positions. In general, the grandmaster proceeds by attempting to strengthen his or her position by gaining control of the center squares, by providing mobility for his or her pieces, by cramping the opponent's position, and so forth.

A computer that can generate a game tree of, say, a maximum of ten moves must first look for a win. But failing that, it must look to better its position in a manner similar to that used by a grandmaster. One way to program this capability into a computer is to assign a value to each position and to have the computer choose the position with the highest value.

The Minimax Method

The most common way of programming values into computer games is called the *minimax method*. The value of each node to a player is the maximum values of its children. When the opponent moves, the value of each node (to the first player) is the minimum of the first player's children. The figure below shows a minimax tree that contains moves for two players.

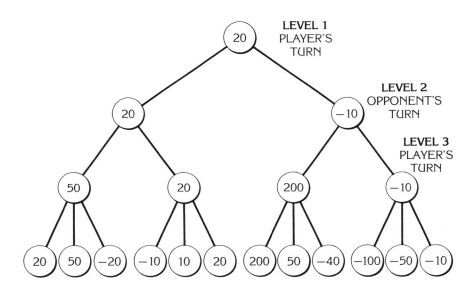

The first level represents the first player's move. This player has two choices. The value of the first level is the maximum of the values of the first player's children (20). The second level represents the opponent's move. (The value of each node in which the opponent moves is the minimum of the first player's children.) The third level again represents the first player's move. (The value of each node is the maximum of its children.) All values on these levels are determined by traveling down the tree and traveling back up. Therefore, they are called *backed-up values.*

Determining the value of each position without generating a complete tree is the intelligent part of the program. This part relies on the human-like abilities to take educated guesses, to make judgments, and to evaluate risks. Here the expert's knowledge must be programmed in. A chess expert evaluates positions in many ways. A computer evaluates positions by giving them numerical values. For example, all of the following are advantages that provide nodes with high values:

1. *Control of the four center squares.* This is considered important in chess. Each square is given a value.
2. *Good mobility of pieces.* Open diagonals and ranks and files provide high values to nodes in which they are present.
3. *More and/or better pieces.*
4. *Opportunity to advance a pawn.* A pawn is promoted to a better piece when it reaches the last square.
5. *More available moves.*

Of course, many of these criteria must be evaluated in terms of the board position as a whole. Some positions that may be good at certain times may be very bad at others. For example, an unprotected pawn would not be valuable even near its final advancement square. Determining the value of any given position is one of the hardest parts of any game program. The ability to successfully evaluate a position is the most important measure of a human or computer game player's expertise.

Players must also evaluate how much search is warranted by a given position. A computer decides this with a routine that determines if a node is a *terminal node,* which the program will not expand further. Here is an example of a routine for defining a terminal node:

1. In expanding the tree for the first five levels, a terminal node is one in which a win, loss, or draw is discovered.
2. In the sixth through ninth levels, a terminal node is a dead position, a position in which a) a piece cannot be captured, b) check is not possible, and c) a pawn will not be promoted.

3. The tenth level is always a terminal node.

The procedure for evaluating a position in minimax depth-first search without generating the entire tree is as follows:

1. The current position is called the root.

2. One child is tested to see if it is to be treated as a terminal node. If so, it is evaluated according to the programmed standards.

3. If the child is not a terminal, it is tested until a terminal node is reached.

4. Once a terminal node is reached, it is evaluated. The value is backed up to the second-level node (first node after the root). In other words, this node then receives the value of the terminal child.

5. To save computer memory, the entire tree below the second level is erased.

6. A second child from the second level is generated. Once a terminal is found, the value is backed up and is compared with the value currently assigned to the second level. If this new value is higher, it replaces the value, and the second level is assigned the new value. Again, everything except the value on the second level is erased.

In this way, the program receives a value for all second-level nodes and chooses the node with the highest value.

In some cases, when computer memory capacity allows, the entire game tree is not erased until a move is decided. This allows the program to go back and expand certain nodes further if the situation warrants. One example of such a situation is when nodes do not yield a positive number. Because usually one player wins and one loses, it is apparent that players do not always move to positions that are favorable. The playing strength of a program, however, can be measured by how often it is able to discover and play to these favorable positions. Here are some of the most important abilities that make this possible:

1. The ability to correctly determine the point value of a given position. The human chess expert must provide the computer engineer with a means of evaluating positions. This ability in human and machine chess players is the most important in determining how well a game must be played to win.

2. The abilities to determine when to cease a search—that is, once a terminal node has been found—and to determine in which areas a search should be expanded. A good chess program knows which positions are not important and which are potentially favorable or hazardous to explore.

The Alpha-Beta Method

Humans use rules of thumb to make these decisions; machines use heuristics. Besides the heuristics discussed above, another important one is called the *alpha-beta method*.

In chess, a parent node always has a child that represents a position in which it is the other player's turn to move. The following figure shows a position in which A represents the first player's turn to move. The position has a value of 10, which it received from backing up from node B. Notice that node B received its value from the minimum of its children, which is 10 (from node F). After expanding along branch 1, the program then must continue to expand, this time along branch 2 to C. This has the value of 8, which it received from node G. We know that the value will never be higher than 8 because it must equal the minimum of the children. So, this value cannot affect the value of A, which is already higher than 8. Therefore, further search on C is not necessary.

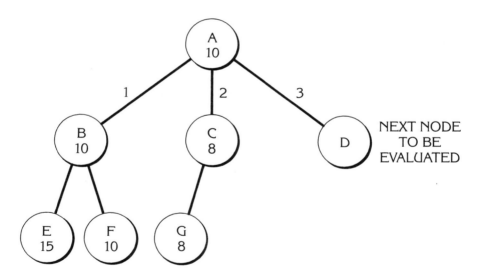

This is an *alpha cutoff*: If a child has a partially backed-up value that is less than its parent's, further evaluation need not be done.

The alpha-beta method is a heuristic that can be used with many different games. Most often, however, a heuristic is confined to its specific game. A common heuristic is the ranking of all possible moves according to the possibility of their achieving high scores. The computer then examines the top ten or so of these moves. There are many ways to determine these *plausibility values.* In general, the rules for determining plausibility values are the same as those that determine the values of the nodes. The only difference is in how they are used.

The three preceding chapters show that intelligent behavior is not as mysterious as it seems. Intelligent behavior can be defined by rules that can be represented in symbolic, computable language. The progress of AI is determined by the ability of researchers to discover these rules.

The development of the programs in the next two chapters, while not leading to direct practical uses, has provided important insights that have assisted in many other projects.

· 14 ·

General Problem
Solver (GPS)

Human intelligence is characterized by its ability to solve many different kinds of problems. AI programs have generally been built to function in limited universes of problem solving and knowledge. They are much like *idiot savants*—mentally defective people who exhibit exceptional skill or brilliance in some limited field. While development of even relatively simple, problem-specific AI systems is full of obstacles, imagine how much more difficult it is to develop systems that can deal with many different kinds of problems. But these systems must be developed if the ultimate hope of some AI researchers is to be realized. This hope—though not necessarily that of any specific research center—is to develop software and hardware (including robots) that can function in the world at least as competently as humans.

Much early work has been done on producing a general problem solver (GPS). Research in this area began in the early 1950s; in 1957, A. Newell, J.C. Shaw, and H.A. Simon produced the first GPS. Work continued throughout the 1950s and 1960s and into the 1970s; recently, though, AI technology advances that have resulted in the production of systems that can work on real-world problems have lessened the interest in this more theoretical area of study. However, a detailed look at the subject is valuable for two reasons: First, we can shed some light on the processes through which problems are solved; second, we can provide clues as to how such processes can be programmed into a computer. Many practical AI programs in use have incorporated concepts learned in the development of general problem solvers.

COMPONENTS OF A GPS

A GPS must have three parts. First, it must have a means of receiving information from the external world (either through user input or through a perception system). If user input is to be utilized in any workable system, some sort of natural-language interface is necessary. Second, the GPS must have a means of internally representing that information. Third, the GPS must have a problem-solving apparatus. We have discussed the first and second parts earlier, so we will confine our discussion to the nature of the general problem-solving apparatus as it exists in the original GPS.

The GPS solves problems by utilizing a series of goals that include the desired result as well as the information required to carry out the solving of the problem. The problem-solving information includes the current situation, the goal situation (the desired outcome), and a memory of all previous attempts to alter the current situation into the goal situation. GPS uses four types of goals:

1. *Transform object A into object B.* For example, a traveler wants to get from point A to point B. The traveler's current situation is point A. The goal is to change the current situation to point B.

2. *Reduce different D on object A.* Our traveler might not be able to transform the current situation into the goal situation in one fell swoop; rather, he or she may need to first reduce the difference between the two states.

3. *Apply operator Q on object A.* This goal measures the effect of operators on the current state. "DRIVE FIVE MILES NORTH" is an example of an operator.

4. *Select elements of set S that best fulfill criterion C.* The purpose of this goal is to match objects.

These four goals have been sufficient in solving many classes of problems. The list, however, is not meant to imply that all reasoning can be encompassed by it. The method of achieving the goals is determined by a *problem-solving executive.* Here are a few examples of the routines contained within the problem-solving executive:

1. *A primitive routine or subroutine:* A one-step solution.

2. *Sequential method:* A list of operations carried out in a fixed order. The only conditional aspect of this method is that the sequence can be terminated partway through the operation.

3. *Signal list:* A conditional list of operations, the signal list is programmed as a set of if/then pairs. One operation is paired to each cur-

rent situation. Whenever the program comes upon a current situation for which it has a match, it will carry out the operation contained in that match. If it does not have a particular current situation in its data base, it will not perform an operation.

4. *Goal-schema method:* Constructs a goal stated in terms of the current situation.

5. *Generate-and-test method:* Generates all possible elements and tests them against certain criteria. The first element that meets all of the criteria is selected.

The problem-solving executive has the job of applying and evaluating all objects and goals. Its functions are method selection, goal recognition, goal evaluation, object recognition, object evaluation, goal selection, and attempt recording.

1. *Method selection:* This function is accomplished through a discrimination tree, similar to a search tree. The current state is the root of the tree. The problem-solving executive searches the tree for the path from the current state to the goal state. It then finds the method or methods that lead there and selects them.

2. *Goal recognition:* This compares the specific goal of the problem with the list of goals in the data base and also uses a discrimination tree. Each node of the tree represents a different data structure. The program compares the goal to each of the nodes until it hits a terminal node that represents the data structures filed in the program. When the program reaches the terminal node, it has a match.

3. *Goal evaluation:* This function rejects goals from immediate consideration. However, the rejected goals do not become part of the search tree; thus, the program can generate them later if other attempts at finding a solution fail. Goals are rejected for one of two reasons. The goal may have a supergoal (an expanded routine) that is easier than its subgoals. (If subgoals are not easier than the overall goal, then the routine is probably illogical.) Or, second, problem solving tends to progress from the difficult to the easy. (GPS will tentatively reject any goals that do not fall into this pattern.)

4. *Object recognition:* This process is similar to goal recognition. It uses a discrimination tree to match the specific (e.g., John Brown) with the general (e.g., man). Its main purpose is to make goal recognition easier. As objects are stored in the program by name, reducing the number of names to general categories reduces the amount of search time.

5. *Object evaluation:* Certain objects along a search may be considered undesirable. This evaluation assists in guiding the search.

6. *Goal selection:* Although complicated goal selection is accomplished by the procedures discussed above, some time is saved by having the problem-solving executive select simple goals.

7. *Attempt recording:* Before abandoning a goal that does not lead to a satisfactory result, the problem-solving executive records information about the attempt so that the route will not be followed again. Also recorded is information on whether all routes on a specific tree have been expanded or if the search has ended for some other reason.

There are a number of methods that GPS uses in achieving goals. A complete description is beyond the scope of this book, but we will touch on a few:

1. *Difference matching:* When two data types are in the GPS data file, the program attempts to define the difference. The GPS determines the difference between the two data types by breaking them down into components and by then attempting to match their component parts. If the difference can be removed with an immediate operator, that operator is applied during the match. If the difference is eliminated, then the match is made.

2. *Difference reduction:* Achieves the goal by reducing the difference between the data structure that represents the current situation and that which represents the goal situation.

3. *Form operator:* Most operators can be applied only to certain objects. One method for achieving a correct match is by ensuring that the form of the object is the same as the form of the operator.

4. *Trying old goals:* If all else fails, the program returns to its past attempts. It looks for a route that has not been exhausted (according to other criteria) and expands it further.

There are four different data structures in the GPS. They correspond to four aspects of a task: objects, operators, goals, and differences.

1. An object may be represented by a tree structure that completely defines the object (e.g., the current situation) or by a list of constraints that define the object.

2. Operators are represented by tests and by the transformations that result from the tests.

3. Goals, as described earlier, contain all the information (i.e., the rules) for solving problems. The only goal given in the initial representation of the problem is the *top goal*. This contains the specifications of the task.

4. Differences are data structures that contain information about the types of differences, the values of the differences, and the nodes in which differences are found.

GPS APPLICATIONS

Now that we have a basic understanding of the workings of GPS, let's look at a few "applications."

Monkey Task

McCarthy invented Monkey Task. It is admittedly an easy problem for humans to solve, but it helps to show how a GPS works. The task is based on some work with primate intelligence. A monkey, some bananas, and a box are in a cage. The bananas hang from a rope attached to the top of the cage and are out of the monkey's grasp. The monkey wants the bananas. It must, of course, move the box under the bananas, climb on top of the box, and reach up.

The general goal (the top goal) is to transform the initial object into the desired object. The initial object is defined as a) monkey is in place 1, b) box is in place 2, c) monkey's hands are empty. The desired object is that the monkey has the bananas in its hands. The four possible operators are all performed by the monkey. It can a) climb on the box, b) walk, c) move the box, and d) get the bananas. Each operator has certain pretests (that is, conditions under which it can occur) and moves (that is, what happens when the pretests occur). The pretest for "get the bananas" ensures that the box is under the bananas and that the monkey is on the box. The result of "get the bananas" is "bananas = contents of monkey's hand." Three possible differences describe the location of the monkey, the location of the box, and the contents of the monkey's hands. The program solves the problem as follows:

1. It tries to reach the bananas in the original configuration by applying the "get the bananas" operator. It fails because that configuration does not satisfy the "get the bananas" criteria that the box be under the bananas and that the monkey be on the box.

2. The monkey cannot move the box under the bananas when the monkey is away from the box. So, to lessen the difference, the program has the monkey walk to the box.

3. The monkey moves the box under the bananas but finds that it still cannot get the bananas because it is not standing on the box.

4. The monkey climbs on the box.

5. And finally, the monkey gets the bananas.

Letter-Series Completion

A more difficult task performed by GPS is the completion of a series of letters. This is the familiar aptitude test question in which the test taker must find the last letters in a series. Here is an example of an incomplete series:

B C B D B E – –

The task is, of course, to fill in the blanks by finding the relationship among the previous letters in the series and by extending that relationship to the blanks. To do this, the program must be given information about relationships among letters. It must also be given a hierarchy of complexity of these relationships, because the program must assign the simplest relationship available. This might not seem obvious at first because humans tend naturally to find the simplest relationship first. This tendency leads us to assign the letters B and F to the blanks above. But a more complex relationship might exist, and the blanks could be filled in with the letters B and C, as in:

B C B D B E B C B D B E B C B D B E . . .

Here are the relationships given GPS:

1. *Same:* Two letters are identical. B is the same as B, for example.
2. *Next:* A letter follows another letter in the alphabet. C is next after B, for example.
3. *Next after next:* M is "next after next" after K, for example.
4. *Predecessor:* D is the predecessor of E, for example.

Simplicity of letter patterns is defined by this hierarchy of relationships as well as by the proximity of letters. If two pairs of letters have the same relationships, the operative pair of letters is the one that is separated by fewer letters.

The program begins at the first (leftmost) letter (B, in our example). It first searches for a "same" relationship, which it discovers in the third letter in the series. The current situation (the letter being worked on) now becomes that third letter. The program again searches for a "same" and finds it in the fifth letter. It jumps to the fifth letter and searches for a "same" in the seventh letter. Finding the seventh position blank, it assigns B to that position (using the "same" relationship). Not having any more letters to analyze, the program jumps back to the second letter of the series, because this is the leftmost letter not yet examined. It first searches for a "same" among the unanalyzed letters. Not finding any, it searches for a "next," which it finds in the fourth letter. It moves now to the fourth letter and looks for a "next" in the sixth letter, which it finds. At the sixth letter, it looks for a "next" in the eighth letter. Not finding any, it places an F (using the "next" relationship) in that blank.

Three-Coin Puzzle

Three coins are on a table. The first and third show tails, and the second shows heads. The object is to have all three coins show the same face—either heads or tails. Exactly three moves (no less) are allowed. Each move consists of turning over two coins at a time.

Here is an outline of how the problem was represented to GPS:

1. *Top goal:* To transform the initial object into the desired object.
2. *Initial object:* Coin 1 = bottom heads, top tails; coin 2 = bottom tails, top heads; coin 3 = bottom heads, top tails. Three moves remain.
3. *Desired object:* The top of coin 2 = the top of coin 3; the top of coin 3 = the top of coin 1; zero moves remain.
4. *Operator:* Flip (that is, move the bottom of coin x to the top of coin x) two coins; decrease move count by one.

GPS proceeds by determining the difference between the current coin and the next coin. And it applies the "flip two coins" operator to lessen the difference. In its successful solution to the problem, the GPS begins by determining the difference between coin 2 and coin 3. It discovers the difference and attempts to reduce that difference by applying the "flip two coins" operator (the only one available to it). So, it flips over coins 1 and 2. It now moves on to coin 3 and notices that the position of this coin does not equal that of coin 1, so it flips over coins 1 and 3. Finally, it notices that coins 1 and 3 do not equal each other, so it flips over coins 1 and 2.

THE USEFULNESS OF GPS

The value of GPS is first in proving that a computer can solve many different kinds of problems and second in beginning a study of the kind of formalization that is needed to interpret problems into symbols that can be computed.

This study has been useful in many areas of AI research, especially in expert systems. Most expert systems consist of two separate parts: a natural-language interpreter and a problem solver. But whether the problem is formalized by the user or by an automatic programmer (the NL system), the techniques of formalization remain the same.

The main difference between an expert system and the GPS is that the expert system must carry with it a large data base of knowledge, while the GPS is like a novice whose work on a problem requires intelligence but very little knowledge. In most cases, the knowledge needed to complete any problem can be conveyed in less than one paragraph. Although this lack of knowledge causes the GPS to remain in the realm of study and not to move into the business world, many of the heuristic methods used in the GPS can be applied to the problem of gaining access to a huge, disjointed data base.

Even in the area of pure problem solving, the GPS lacks the ability to solve many different kinds of problems. The hope of developing a machine that can solve diverse problems as a human can remains unfulfilled.

One suggested solution is to design a program containing an enormous array of problem-solving techniques. The "brains" of this program would be a diagnostic routine (the "Big Switch" method) that matches the problem with the correct solving routine. There are questions, however, as to whether such a system is a true general problem solver. At one extreme, a system might have so many different methods (perhaps one for each problem) that the diagnostic router does little more than name the problem. Such a system cannot honestly be considered a single-problem solver; it is many problem solvers within one box. So, it would lose its claim as being a general problem solver.

One test for determining if a system is a general problem solver is in how that system uses its problem-solving techniques. If each technique is used as a whole for every problem, the problem solver is probably a specific (and not a general) problem solver. But if a problem solver can break a problem down into parts, and each part can be attacked by different routines that are found in different parts of the program, so that any given problem might be solved by any number of different combinations of routines, then that is a general problem solver.

A true general problem solver would be very useful in eliminating the redundancy and expense in building a system with a large number of integrated routines for different problems.

The GPS has provided AI researchers with answers to many questions about machine *and* human problem solving. It has also contributed to the understanding of generality in problem solving. Although general problem solvers are not on the current agendas of most AI researchers, they are certainly a hope for the future.

▪ 15 ▪

Learning Systems

Eventually, AI machines will be able to learn. Lack of this ability greatly increases development costs and time and makes some applications almost impossible. Developers are faced with the choice of producing machines applicable to only one industry (sometimes to one company) or of installing gigantic data bases of information—much of which will not be used by any one user. The ideal machine would come with a minimum amount of preinstalled general information. More information would be learned on the job. This type of system could be mass-produced; it would thus become accessible to more than a few wealthy corporations.

BRAIN-BASED LEARNING SYSTEMS

Many learning systems, especially early ones, are based on the physiological structure of the brain. Developers of these systems believe that the brain is very much like a computer that contains a relational data base. For example, in a relational data base, each piece of data contains information as to the addresses of other pieces of data. Often, those pieces are stored, one to one, as a list. The solving of a problem comes to the thinker by association—one fact or piece of data leading to the next. We refer to this method of information processing in a computer as a *looping structure*.

137

There is anatomical evidence that the brain processes information in a looping path. Covering the brain is the cerebral cortex, which is connected to the much smaller thalamus (a bundle of nerve cells). When information is received from sensory nerves, it is transmitted first to the thalamus, then to the cortex, where it is processed. It then returns to the thalamus. The information is then processed further and is returned to the cortex. The operation is repeated several times. It is believed that at each pass from the thalamus to the cortex, the information is refined and categorized, and related data is retrieved and attached to it. This back-and-forth movement, along with the possible data retrieval that may be associated with it, is similar to the looping structure in relational data bases.

The cerebral cortex-thalamus loop is only one example of this type of structure in the brain. Many other such loops exist. For example, the cortex transmits to the cerebellum, which transmits to the thalamus, which transmits back to the cortex.

Because processing performed on data received from the sensory nerves is the most easily studied, and also because these loops are most likely to yield information on the building of learning systems, early AI research has focused on these pathways. The cerebellum constantly receives input information via mossy fibers at the rate of 20 to 30 charges a second—even when few sensory or muscular stimuli are present. The information may come from the cerebral cortex, which has received data from the thalamus. Or the data may arrive from parts of the body. Receptor organs in muscles, joints, and skin relay information. When someone touches our hands, or when we feel cold or heat, we register that information through the mossy fiber network. Even coordination is made possible through these communicators, because the extent of muscle contraction or relaxation is also conveyed.

Fibers may branch off, each branch ending in a number of terminals, where the synapse (the gap through which electrical charges jump) is found. This synapse is called a rosette. Each branch of a mossy fiber may contain 20 to 50 rosettes. Each fiber, considering all its branches, may contain hundreds of rosettes. Each piece of data is sent along its route to the area responsible for its processing.

At each rosette, branching continues to the granule cells. These are the most numerous cells in the brain, and each rosette may come in contact with about 20 granule cells. Each granule cell rises (through an axon) toward the surface of the cortex. When the granule cell reaches the surface, it branches off in two directions and makes contact with other brain cells called Purkinje cells, basket cells, stellate cells, and Golgi cells.

Another type of input fiber is the climbing fiber. Climbing fibers seem to respond more to external stimuli than to purposeful activity.

Electrical spikes in climbing fibers, for example, appear when the skin is pinched but not when a muscle jerks as a result of being pinched. As with mossy fibers, climbing fibers branch out and make contact with other cells. They are distinguished from mossy fibers, though, by their dramatic, violent spikes of electrical activity.

Perception

The first computer program and system to be designed around the model of the brain were developed in the 1960s by F. Rosenblatt. Called Perception, the system consisted of processor cells that accepted and gave electrical impulses of various strengths. When a cell receives input, it measures the strength of the input against a predetermined threshold. If the strength of the input exceeds the threshold, the cell fires; if it does not, the cell does nothing.

The input apparatus for Perception was modeled after the eye, and the system was to be a pattern-recognition system that learns. In the eye, patterns are presented to a layer of sensory cells, the retina. Information from the retina is passed on to a layer of associative cells that transfer the pattern. It is possible that these associative cells perform a feature-determination activity on the input, but they may simply pass the information on randomly. These associative cells then pass the input through synapses to response cells. The strength of the electrical activity over these synapses varies with the strength of the signal and possibly with some internal manipulation of the data by the associative cells themselves. The response cells either fire or do not fire, a reaction based on the strength of the charge received from the associative cells. This firing or not firing is passed on to the brain, which recognizes the pattern in the input.

Perception also has light-sensitive cells. The information they pick up is passed to a group of associative cells. The associative cells then pass their information (that is, the strengths of stimuli) along to response cells. If the strength of a stimuli is high enough—as measured by the programmed threshold—the response cell will recognize it. If it is not strong enough, the response cell will ignore it. The threshold can be automatically changed by the program; this is the learning part of the system.

Perception was given a set of input patterns and was instructed that some patterns were to be coded class 1 and others class 0. The more times the program practiced the procedure, the fewer classification errors it made. Eventually, the program achieved complete accuracy.

The following figure shows the basic working of Perception. The outer part of the apparatus is made up of light-sensing cells. Each of these cells is either stimulated or not stimulated. When a cell is stimulated, it releases a +1 charge to the associative cell; when a cell is not being stimulated, it releases a −1 charge. The associative cells then pass on the total input value to evaluators (adjustable weight cells). If the value received by the adjustable weight cells is sufficiently high, the information is passed on to response cells; if it is not high enough, information is not passed on.

DIAGRAM PERCEPTION

Weights
Adjustable

| Sensory Cells | Associate Cells | Adjustable Weights | Response Cells |

As noted, all work in the learning process is carried on by changing the values in the adjustable weight cells. These values are changed automatically by the program according to the following rules:

1. If a pattern is incorrectly classified (as class 0 when it should be class 1), increase all weights (or decrease thresholds) coming from active associative cells.
2. If a pattern is incorrectly classified (as class 1 when it should be class 0), decrease all weights (or raise thresholds) coming from active associative cells.

3. If a pattern is correctly identified, do not change weights or thresholds.

Increasing or decreasing weights or values of received data is, in general, an important part of all learning systems. It is very close, if not identical, to the way humans learn to discriminate different objects. In distinguishing, for example, a car from a truck, we must decrease the weight of factors such as speed, carbon monoxide exhaust, and the presence of a steering wheel—all of which appear in both—and we must increase the weight factors such as the number of tires, the size, the weight, and so forth.

Perception has worked well on simple patterns, but as complexity increases, the ability of Perception quickly decreases to nearly zero. It is impossible to store in a manageable machine the number of cells required to function with a complex pattern. And the number of required cells increases rapidly with even a small increase in the complexity of the pattern.

A change that might improve Perception is the recoding of information received from one sensory cell into 100 associative cells. This version of Perception has been called Expansion Recorder Perception. As it would allow for a lot of redundancy in the system, severe restrictions can be placed on the associative cells without loss of accuracy. For example, only one percent of the associative cells is allowed to be active for any given input. This not only decreases the number of necessary associative cells, but also makes for faster learning. Because any given associative cell participates in only one percent of any classification, its adjustable weight would not need to be changed as frequently.

Percy

In the 1970s, another program was developed to exhibit learning. It is called Percy. The purpose of the project was to develop guidelines for building a system that can interact with an environment while not having an internal representation of that environment. The need for this type of system is evident. First, environmental details may be too varied to be represented. (We have already discussed the problem of a robot moving around a cluttered construction site.) Second, even when environmental details can be predicted, the hardware necessary for storing hundreds of facts either may not exist or may be too cumbersome or expensive.

Percy has a hierarchical organization that allows for a task-oriented context for its interactions with the environment. Percy is a robot that is simulated on a computer. Its task is to build a nest. Its environment includes the nest, nest-building material, food, walls, and landmarks. The nest and nest-building material are stationary. The food and Percy move around. To eat, Percy must capture and destroy the food. The walls, as well as the nest, are obstacles around which Percy must navigate. Landmarks can be seen from any distance, but they must be in Percy's angle of vision and they must not be blocked by other objects if they are to be seen. Landmarks help Percy to find the nest, nest-building material, and food.

Percy builds the nest by making trips to and from the nest material; it brings the material to the nest. Eight trips are necessary to complete the operation. At the same time, Percy must catch food to retain enough strength to complete the task. It doesn't have to eat on every trip, but if it doesn't make good decisions about when to begin to look for food, it may starve, and the task will not be completed successfully. At any point, the decision either to work on the nest or to look for food causes a conflict, because each task takes time away from the other.

Percy is able to determine if it is satisfied or not—and its degree of satisfaction becomes the measure of its success. Things that decrease its satisfaction are being behind schedule in the nest building and being hungry. Each decision it makes is based on the need to increase its satisfaction. But there is no programmed method of accomplishing this. At each point, its decision is based on what has worked in the past. However, Percy cannot recall the exact sequence of decisions that led to success in the past, because to do this would simplify its job too much—it wouldn't be learning; it would just be copying. Also, the goal is to find out if Percy can string together good decisions in a logical manner.

When the process starts, Percy builds its nest. Then Percy is returned to the beginning state, and the task begins again. It performs the task more efficiently with each practice run.

Here is a description of part of a session with Percy:

1. It has just placed some nest material in a nest.
2. It sights a landmark that represents more nest material.
3. It backs away from the nest and moves around it until it has a clear view of the landmark.
4. It moves toward the landmark.
5. When it is near the landmark, it turns sideways and continues to move, crablike, until it is within arm's length of the material.
6. Its arm reaches out, grasps some material, and places the material on its back.
7. It circles around until a nest landmark comes into view.

8. It heads toward the landmark, again turning sideways when it draws near.

9. However, the particular nest it has approached is already filled with material. Percy now does a ritual dance that is repeated at any filled nest site. Percy dances by moving one step toward the site and by then turning away from and circling the site. (This dance was not programmed into Percy on purpose.)

10. The dance brings Percy nearer to the next site, which is also filled. So the dance is repeated. On the third try Percy finds an empty nest site.

11. When it is arm's length from this site, Percy removes the material from its back and deposits it at the site.

12. On the next trip, it catches food first. On the way back from catching food, it picks up more material.

Each activity has a purpose. The ritual dance, which is similar to rituals performed in nature, would be difficult to remove from the program.

Percy has to make many decisions during the course of its task, the most important being whether to hunt for food or to spend time in nest building. Each decision is based on a satisfaction value. Satisfaction is based on two factors: the time since Percy last ate and the time since it last added to its nest. Learning takes place by automatic adjustment of the factors involved in the satisfaction value.

To be more specific, the satisfaction at any point is an average of two quantities—the measure of the immediately past satisfaction and the satisfaction expected from the outcome of the immediate situation. So, when Percy is eating, the first would be low because it would have been hungry and would not have been very satisfied. But the second quantity would be high, because Percy would not be hungry after the current situation (that is, after eating).

Percy self-adjusts (that is, it learns). It adjusts the relative importance it places on each satisfaction value. Percy learns which of the two drives it should respond to at any given time while still being satisfactorily set on the other drive.

A Game-Playing Program That Learns

A.G. Bell has developed a program that plays games better with experience. The game is called Kalah. Its description and rules are as follows.

The board appears below. The circles and ovals are depressions in the board. The dots represent playing pieces. The game begins with an equal number of playing pieces in each depression. The difficulty of the game is varied by adding or lessening the number of pieces with which each player begins.

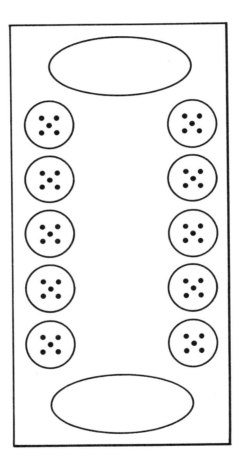

The ovals are called kalahs. The kalah to a player's right belongs to that player. First, a player empties one depression, and, starting to its right, distributes the pieces one in each depression, continuing if necessary to the opponent's depressions. When the player gets to his or her kalah, one piece is dropped in there as well. Once a piece is in the kalah, it is never removed. The only depression a player passes over is the opponent's kalah. The object of the game is to get more pieces into one's own depression than the opponent gets into his or her depression.

The program has four parts: a list of legal moves, a minimax evaluation process, memory plus backtracking, and a compression mechanism to limit the size of the memory as the program learns. We will concern ourselves here only with the third and fourth functions, because they are the ones that deal with learning.

Memory is made up of game positions that led to a known outcome. As the program has no memory before the first game, it relies entirely on the minimax problem-solving method. Eventually, the program discovers that it will win (or lose) within the next 1.5 moves. If it will win, it stores that information in its memory as a position to aim for. If it will lose, it tries to find out why and, in the process, builds up its store of winning and losing positions. Thus, more progress is made when a position is lost than when it is won.

To discover why it will lose, the program returns up the branches of the game tree. It evaluates the position of the parent of its present position. It determines if any of the siblings of its present (losing) position would possibly fare better for the program. If not, it moves further up the game tree.

The memory of the program is conserved in two ways. First, only information that is necessary to the process of the game is included. If memory of the contents of certain depressions is not necessary to understanding why a given position is a win or loss, that information is erased. Second, if winning information is contained further up a game tree, all nodes below this information are erased.

Obviously, the further a player gets from a real win, the more likely it is that some unforeseen move or blunder will cause a result that the player does not expect. So, the program is made to run on a 90-percent accuracy basis. That is, if a given position turns into a winning (or losing) position at least 90 percent of the time, that position will be considered a win (or loss). Moves that occur after that position are not kept in the computer's memory.

A Pleasure-Seeking Program

Another learning program acts as a pleasure-seeking rat in a cage does. It was developed by J.E. Doran. It is something like the Percy program, but it is more sophisticated. The environment in which the simulated automaton travels, however, is more complicated and is closer to real-world situations.

Doran describes the situation as being similar to that in which a family tries to find a way home by constantly taking busier and busier thoroughfares because they know they live on a very busy street. At first, the family may walk in circles and then set off in another direction. Eventually, they find their way home. The next time they are taken from their home and are abandoned, they are able to find a more direct route home.

The actual situation is closer to that of a rat in a cage. The rat needs two things: to be warm and to be fed. It lies in a warm nest. When it gets hungry, it ventures out to find some food. When it has eaten, it returns to the next. After each session, the rat maneuvers faster and more efficiently, taking fewer blind alleys and more direct routes.

Conclusion

Viewing in isolation the systems described in this chapter, it might seem that AI researchers have nothing better to do than to play with automated creatures. But AI breakthroughs come from such research. Once the technology succeeds with these small prototypes, larger learning systems may be possible. But here, as in many other areas of AI, there is no proof that such systems will ever exist. The technology gained from these programs has so far not been substantial enough to justify optimism.

▪ FOUR ▪

THINKING ABOUT AI

· 16 ·

Psychological Foundations

AI research has generally focused on developing machines that can reason through methods that humans are perceived to use in solving problems. But not all human problem solving or decision making is based on methods that can be easily observed. Many solutions are found through intuition and creativity. And many decisions are based on emotional considerations.

Can computers be made to love, hate, show compassion, or be creative? And, perhaps more important, should they? Certainly these goals cannot be high on the agenda of a science that has not yet been able to make a computer that can walk around in a nonstructured environment. But many researchers feel that, somewhere along the line, the psychological qualities of human behavior must be programmed into machines.

WHY PROGRAM EMOTIONS?

The researchers' reasons fall into three categories. First, there is the "we must build it because it is there" reason. Because psychological qualities are part of human intelligence, they should be incorporated into a machine that is built to mimic human intelligence. This says little about how such machines can benefit humans. But in the philosophical debate over whether a machine can truly be made to think, proving

149

that a machine can have emotions and creativity would be strong evidence for a positive answer.

Second, the presence of emotions and creativity in humans suggests that there must be a reason for their existence. If emotions and creativity were maladaptive, they would have evolved out of the species. And the fact that many of the great thinkers and leaders of the world are emotional, creative people lends support to the importance of those qualities. For a machine to be able to make decisions on a par with those of these thinkers, it must be programmed to make use of psychological factors.

Third, because the computer will have to function in the real world and interact with and understand humans, both emotional responses and emotional understanding will be necessary. For example, to understand that a person might fight for honor might be difficult for a computer unless it understands emotions. A computer may need to make decisions for its human master, decisions based on emotional responses of love, hate, or compassion.

PROGRAMMING EMOTIONS

Present-day machines are unemotional rationalists. Emotions, however, are based on rules—certain things make us angry, other things make us frightened. There is no reason to believe that these rules cannot be coded and computed.

Furthermore, one theory holds that emotions may be products of the human physical "machine"—the brain and the nervous system. Emotions are output, not input. A specific brain section is responsible for receiving sensory input of a certain kind and for issuing a corresponding emotion at a specific intensity. One part of the brain computes pleasure and contentment, another fear, another sexual arousal, another pain. There are 53 such emotional computation centers linked together by 35 major nerve bundles. The entire network of centers and nerve bundles is called the limbic system. The limbic system also controls thirst, hunger, and body cycles (such as sleep) and aids in storing sensory information into memory. This last function works with emotional output. Any experience that has a strong emotion attached to it will have a strong memory connection.

Input to the limbic system consists of data that has already been processed by other parts of the brain. Images are recognized and are attached to associated memory; their significance is also determined. If man A views, for example, man B walking toward him in a way that, because of associated memories, seems threatening, those associated memories will be attached to the emotion of fear. A confidence factor is also included in the output. It is a measure of how confident a person is that his or her emotional output is appropriate—and it is usually represented by a strengthening or weakening of the output signal.

Limbic system processing is based on contextual understanding of a situation. For example, a person would probably not be afraid of a nip from his or her own dog, but he or she might be afraid of a nip from a strange dog. And the context is not only the present situation; it is also the memories of many past situations. If a person has always had nonthreatening experiences with dogs, that person might find it difficult to believe that any one dog could be dangerous. And so, the fear that might normally arise when a person encounters a dog would be slow in developing.

Response to any given stimuli depends on a number of factors. All of these can be explained by using a series of rules—if/then statements—that can be programmed into a computer. The question is whether humans actually function by these rules. Are we controlled by a program that, although often changing, will always output a certain response to a certain stimulus?

Perhaps the question should not be whether humans are controlled by programs, but whether humans use programs to make decisions. There is little doubt that humans usually do not consciously choose to be afraid or sad or joyful in the same way that they choose to cross a street. Following certain rules or programs will produce certain emotions, but people seem not to be in control of these rules. Even so, people can use them (if unconsciously), and these rules do have an important adaptive function. They provide shortcuts in the decision-making process; they are a means by which a person can protect himself or herself by acting appropriately in any given situation without having to spend time thinking about it. People can choose to change the rules, and with some difficulty they might be successful. Sometimes they may use therapists to help in understanding the programs of their minds and in reprogramming. But the rules are there, no matter if they are discovered by the individual or if they are drawn out by the therapist. So, ironically, here in the emotional center of man, in the one area that many people predict no machine can imitate, is a behavior source that is very closely related to a computer program.

We do not know for sure how the program is built into a human's mind. Some psychologists believe that at least an initial program is transmitted genetically. Others believe that all these rules are programmed at a very young age (say, before the age of five). But however the initial program is installed, it is clear that further programming is done. To described human behavior as a result of programming does not demean the human condition; programmed behavior simply explains an effective means of operating in a world in which a person does not have the time to study each situation and to determine how to react.

One argument against the rule-based nature of human emotions is that there is a higher intelligence or higher spirit that is the motivating and vivifying force. This force is not confined to rule-based behavior; therefore, when humans are under its influence, they are also not so confined. Evidence for this theory can be found in the sudden transformations of people's lives—in other words, in sudden and seemingly automatic reprogramming—brought on by prayer or meditation. We do not know for sure how these transformations take place. But let's look at two possible explanations. One is that transformations occur through the intercession of an external force, such as God. If this is the case, it does not disprove the theory that emotions are rule-based and that they can be programmed. It simply means that there is a force that acts on humans, that changes their behavior, and that does not choose to act in the same way toward machines. But man's ability to receive that force is not intelligence. Transformations may also be said to occur because of quirks in human personalities. These quirks allow people to undergo immediate personality changes, but there is no evidence that such changes are not also rule-based (though governed by rules not yet understood). These rules, once understood, presumably could be programmed.

Programming Beliefs

Although we have scant knowledge as to how people build up the rule systems that govern their behavior and emotions, what we do know seems programmable. For example, a very important part of our emotional makeup is our faiths or beliefs. Beliefs may haphazardly and quickly become part of our programs, but they may be weak at first and may be easily discarded. Actions that confirm our beliefs reinforce them. The more often actions confirm a belief, the stronger that belief becomes. And the stronger a belief, the more resistant it is to change.

This process of assimilating beliefs and of altering them can be easily quantified and thus computed. For example, the number of times a belief (and its strength) must be tested to be assimilated can be determined by clinical tests. Our not being able to predict with high accuracy how any individual will respond to a belief-assimilating routine results from our not knowing all that has gone into that person's program. A computer—a blank slate before being programmed—would be more malleable. Modeling a program on a specific person such that we can predict behavior with 100-percent accuracy is difficult. This is because we cannot know all the rules that have gone into that person's personality. But modeling a program on an average human is certainly possible. Specializing the program so that it would respond as, say, a top-notch salesman or as a politician would is also an option.

We may change our beliefs because of personal experience or because people we respect—or a large number of people that we do not necessarily respect—have a contrary belief. A computer could be given values for different types of people: A person with average knowledge might be valued as 1, a school teacher as 3, and an esteemed scientist as 5. It is easy to imagine a program that would need, say, 15 points to change a weak belief and 50 points to alter a strong belief.

ATTENDING TO THE ENVIRONMENT

Attending to a part of the environment is another function that is important in understanding the world. This function operates on a more primitive level than that on which forming beliefs operates. A multi-purpose robot will not only have to be able to sense the world in general, but at times it must also be able to focus on a specific part of its environment. Attending to the environment involves two activities. First, the robot would have to track a subject that, if not tracked, would disappear from the robot's field of vision. A moving human or robot will encounter—primarily through vision—many objects. While the viewer can allow most of these objects to enter and leave its field of vision—as the viewer or the viewed object moves—it must track certain objects. That is, it must use its sensors to follow the objects until they are no longer important to its task.

Second, the robot must focus on certain objects; it must filter out extraneous details, and it may enlarge its image.

Programming these activities—tracking and focusing—is not difficult. The difficulty arises when a system must decide whether attending to the environment is necessary. The problem becomes even more complicated when the system must attend to more than one object. Should the robot attend to all objects in a limited way? Or should it attend to only one in a complete way?

Because robots are built for specific environments, attending routines must also be built for specific environments. But as robots are built to be used in many different environments, the decisions as to which objects need attending will have to be determined by heuristics built into the programs themselves.

PROGRAMMING IMAGINATION

Another psychological function is imagination. Imagination entails using fragments of memories to construct images in our minds. Sometimes memories remain intact and are relived exactly as they happened. Sometimes we reconstruct events, adding or eliminating elements and guessing how situations would have been different with the introduction of these new elements. Sometimes one person may recall events—either real or fictional—that happened to someone else and may imagine those events as happening to him- or herself.

Imagination is used to make guesses about the real world. A person walks down a road and hears a dog growling. Immediately, the person sees a dog in his or her imagination. Or, a person wants to build a bookcase and imagines doing it, finding shortcuts and pitfalls before actually beginning to work. Through imagination, we can test the world while saving time and materials and without being exposed to dangerous situations.

The ability of programs to make guesses about what would occur under a given set of circumstances can be viewed as rudimentary imagination. In fact, the function of most expert systems can be said to be to provide imaginative solutions to difficult problems.

We can go even a step further in relating computer activity to human activity. We have seen in Chapter 15 that programs can use "pleasure" or "satisfaction" as a means of determining what to do. Designing a program that exhibits pleasure as it "imagines" certain subjects would not be difficult. The computer can "exhibit pleasure" by exploring those imaginings in detail, by repeating them over and over, and by working out all possible variations and ramifications. If a ramification produces a negative emotion, the program would—as a human would—discontinue the negative activity. Using pleasure to determine what to do would be useful to the decision-making capability of a program. If a program needs to work with an imagined subject, the imaginings could help the computer find the best strategies for doing so. If the computer is to work with the subject at another time, it would store in its memory information concerning that subject. Fragments of worked-out situations would become part of the knowledge base of the computer and might be used in the future. Because imaginings are sometimes not related to an immediate problem, and because the goal of imagination is to find the right combination of thoughts that lead to pleasurable emotions, a program with "imagination" could be said to be a daydreamer; it imagines for the sake of pleasure.

CAN CREATIVITY BE PROGRAMMED?

The highest level of human thinking may be creativity. Creativity is the piecing together of information that is already known. We have learned from experience, though, that solutions to problems sometimes seem to come like bolts out of the blue. A person may ponder a problem for hours without finding a solution. But suddenly, as the person relaxes, everything comes together, and the problem is solved. The mechanism by which this happens has been studied extensively, but it is still not understood. We can probably assume, however, that a problem *is* sometimes solved subconsciously.

Can a machine be creative in this manner? In one sense, all machine thinking is performed in this way. (Because we assume, but cannot prove, that a machine is not conscious, we might say that all its thinking is done through subconscious processes.)

Creativity, faiths, emotions, and all other psychological activities can be recognized by their effects. There is no way to know for sure what exactly a person is experiencing. In studying intelligence, it is useless to speculate whether a machine—or a human being—feels exactly as we do when we produce the same external response. The important job for the AI community is to produce machines that can use the adaptive psychological activities that allow people to reason effectively.

· 17 ·

Philosophical Foundations

The purpose of this chapter and the next is to discuss, in the abstract, whether it is possible for machines to think and to possess such human attributes as free will and a sense of aesthetics. As we have seen, machines that think at least as well as humans do do not yet exist. And there is no sure way of predicting whether developers will come up with the right combination of hardware and software to accomplish the feat of producing such machines. However, if we look at the history of science, it seems safe to say that if a given invention can be conceived by a rational person, then the invention can be developed. So, answering the abstract question of whether machines can think will most likely answer the question of whether such machines will ever exist in the flesh.

Of course, developing a machine that can merely think as well as humans would be a monumental waste of time and money. The idea is to develop a machine that can solve problems that are too large for humans. If human thought processes can be simulated by a machine, the ability to surpass human thinking certainly seems not far away. For unless we run up against an impenetrable barrier, there is no reason to believe that scientists can't build a brain, and then a larger and a more perfect one. The trick, though, is to build the first brain.

To determine if machines can think, we must be able to agree on the criteria for making such a determination. But attempting a definition of thinking presents two problems: First, it is difficult to make the definition broad enough to encompass all activities that would generally be called thinking and to not make it so broad so as to render it meaningless; second, it is impossible to observe the process of thinking in humans. Probably the best solution is to assert that 1) humans *do* think, 2) machines *do* think only if they can produce the same results that humans produce when they think.

The Turing Test, mentioned in Chapter 1, has been suggested as one way of testing the thinking ability of a machine. The test is based on a game in which a man or woman is concealed behind a curtain or in a room that is removed from the players. The players ask questions through the curtain or through the door to determine if the concealed person is a man or a woman. The concealed person answers via typewriter or via some other means that does not give away his or her sex. The Turing Test would proceed in a similar fashion, except that the object of the players would be to discover if the concealed "person" is human or a machine. If the "person" is a machine, and if the players are unable to guess this fact, then the machine can be said to think.

This means of determining whether machines can think also provides a means of proving that they can't—without having to describe in detail what it is that machines cannot do. This is very important, because in some cases such a description is impossible to come by. In fact, Turing has argued that if someone claimed that machines could not think because they could not perform a certain thinking function, scientists could then use the same description of that function to build a system to perform it. To be fair, then, to those who believe that machines cannot think, there must be a means of determining that machines cannot think—without describing what they cannot do.

One argument against the possibility of thinking machines comes from Kurt Gödel. In his Incompleteness Theory, he has shown that within any logical system are theories that can neither be proved nor disproved. In other words, certain functions must be performed outside the system. For one system to be able to prove these theories, it must be logically inconsistent. But, because machines must be programmed in a logically consistent manner, they will not be able to function in some areas of thought. Humans, however, are able to incorporate inconsistencies into their thought processes and thus do not suffer from this problem.

The path by which Gödel came to his conclusion involves very complicated processes that are beyond the scope of this book. It is enough to say that many mathematicians agree with him in principle. There, is, however, disagreement as to whether his theory proves the argument that thinking machines cannot be built. For example, here are three replies:

1. Calculating machines are limited in what they can accomplish because they are confined to following logical steps very closely. The logic of these machines allows them to compute at lightning speed, and so logic is both their main asset as well as the cause of their limitation. But human brains also have built-in limitations (for example, they cannot visualize a fourth dimension). Limitations in themselves do not render machines incapable of thinking as humans do.

2. Gödel's argument is that simply providing a system with axioms and rules does not allow it to solve all classes of problems. But, many AI systems contain more than axioms and rules; they can also use heuristics and other techniques that go outside the axioms and rules.

3. Gödel's argument works only on deductive machines that are given rules before "thinking." Current AI research is more concerned with inductive machines, which can alter their structures through their interaction with the environment—a process commonly called learning.

Another proposed criterion for a thinking machine is that it must have the same degree of determinism (or lack thereof) that humans have. Any computer that will always produce C given A and B will be more machine than human. To some extent, this criterion has already been met: Game-playing programs, when confronted with identical positions several times, do not always respond in the same way.

But board positions are not as simple as they may seem. A human or a machine responds differently to the same position because there are determining factors other than position. For example, the player might be using one strategy for one opponent and another strategy for another opponent. Or the progress of the game might lend itself to a specific set of moves. If it were possible, which it obviously is not, to discover all these determining factors, the actions of a human or of a thinking machine might be more predictable. The point is that when a viewer judges something to be unpredictable, this judgment often is a result of the viewer's being unaware of all the factors that went into the "unpredictable" event. And that this seeming unpredictability can, and has been, programmed into computers.

Another aspect of intelligence is aesthetics. Can a machine draw a picture or write a poem? As seen in Chapter 3, a program has already been developed to write original stories. Programming this ability is not as difficult as it might seem. Aesthetic pleasure varies from society to society. What pleases a group of people is determined by rules that art and literature critics are fond of discovering. Programming these rules into a computer is not a difficult problem.

But can a computer spontaneously—and, unprodded by a human—decide to write a poem or draw a picture? The question brings us back to the discussion as to whether computers can have emotions. As we have seen, given a person who has a specific set of emotional responses to specific stimuli, that person's behavior can be programmed into a computer. In Chapter 15, we discussed computers that are motivated by hunger. It is easy to imagine the same program being motivated by a need to create.

Given that computers can mimic human capabilities in intellectual and emotional pursuits, we come to the question of whether a computer can have consciousness. In attempting to answer this question, we must set ground rules for determining consciousness. Whatever these ground rules are, they must be fairly applied to machine and human alike. And as we try to agree on these rules, it becomes evident that there is no way for one person to know from experience if anyone else is also conscious. We must take other people at their words, or we must judge them by their actions. Because these actions are not consciousness—but rather, supposed manifestations of consciousness—and because, as we have seen, it is easy to imagine a non-conscious being acting in a way similar to that of a conscious being, we come to the conclusion that the only conscious act is self-awareness. Self-awareness is the ability of a being to refer to itself, to be able to think "I feel cold" or "I am satisfied."

This self-awareness allows a person to change his or her behavior. A person feels cold or happy or hateful and responds in a manner that is appropriate to his or her behavior pattern. There is no reason to believe that a machine cannot monitor itself and respond in a way that is similar to human behavior. And there is no way to prove or disprove that such a machine is conscious.

At one level, free will is like consciousness—it is perceived only by its owner. It is the ability to choose from among many given alternative actions. But again, one person would be hard pressed to prove that free will exists in someone else.

If free will is the ability to choose from among many different alternatives, there is no doubt that a computer can be so programmed. In fact, because the human psychological makeup (that is, the human program) is generated so haphazardly and is so difficult to alter, we can say that we could develop a computer with fewer "psychological restrictions" and therefore more free will.

Clearly, machines can perform almost any function that people can perform. Programming free will or a sense of aesthetics may be unnecessary for most applications, but aspects of these functions may prove to be useful. The theoretical ability to program these functions shows how closely machines can be made to simulate human minds. And it therefore shows to what extent machines can become our assistants.

· 18 ·

Is AI Attainable?

Artificial intelligence has its share of detractors and naysayers. Some researchers and philosophers claim not only that artificial intelligence has not yet reached its goal of truly simulating human reason—an argument no one can deny—but also that such a goal is unrealistic.

The intellectual leader of this group is Hubert L. Dreyfus, the author of *What Computers Can't Do*. Dreyfus and others believe that AI researchers are basing their hopes on assumptions that are incorrect. Dreyfus sees four such assumptions, some of which we have already discussed:

1. The biological assumption that the brain is physically similar to a computer. Information is processed by the brain in ways that are closely related to the digital (on-off) method used in present-day computers.

2. The psychological assumption that the mind functions according to rules that can be quantified and translated into digital code.

3. The epistemological assumption that all knowledge can be coded into digital form.

4. The ontological assumption that world knowledge can be broken down into independent pieces that are totally situation-free and that can be so programmed into a digital computer.

As these assumptions form the core of AI research, we should look at each closely.

160

THE BIOLOGICAL ASSUMPTION

Neurophysiologists have long known that the brain neurons of the higher animals (including those of humans) fire all-or-nothing bursts of electricity. Many computer scientists and others hope that this proves that the brain functions as a binary computer. If each of those bursts contains one bit of information coded in an on-or-off fashion, perhaps this method of coding can be applied to computers. All we have to do is build a machine that functions mechanically as a brain. Once this is accomplished, information can be input in a way similar to the way information is given to humans. The machine physically based on the human brain would be able to function as the human mind does.

One problem with this assumption is that—despite the electrical bursts—there is no evidence that the brain processes information digitally.

The difference between digital and analog processing is in how the information is obtained and used, not in how it is conveyed. Both a light switch and a variable-speed electric drill receive information through on and off bursts. However, the light simply determines if the current is on or off, while the drill measures the intensity of the signal. If each burst of electricity pulsing through a brain neuron contained the code for a complete bit of information simply by the fact that the neuron is on or off, then the brain would be in fact a binary or digital computer. But it has been discovered that a charge passing through one axon would release an electronic message that would be different from that released through another axon. So, brain activity may consist of thousands of different, finely graded charges emanating from only one initial charge. This seems to show at least that the brain recognizes analog signals. Whether this is so or not, it is certain that the brain cannot be understood simply by studying the individual neurons. And the complex organization of the brain makes constructing such a system impossible.

Finally, even if the brain functioned digitally, it would still be too complex to be duplicated exactly. We are still far from building a machine that can operate heuristically using such a large array of neuron bits. As seen with the Perception program, such a system might be able to provide output similar to the input, but using these random bits to process material so that the output is useful has never been accomplished.

For these reasons, many AI researchers have abandoned the hope of building a human brain and instead are attempting to discover how the mind works. They hope that mind functions, if not brain functions, can be digitally coded.

THE PSYCHOLOGICAL ASSUMPTION

The psychological assumption is that the mind, if not the brain, functions as a digital computer. How the brain stores and processes information is irrelevant. Humans go through two steps in making sense of the material world. First, they translate raw images, sounds, tones, reflections of light, and so on into integrated wholes. For example, a collection of tones becomes a song, a collection of light and dark images becomes a picture, and a collection of lines traced across a screen becomes a television image.

Second, they combine, relate, separate, and otherwise manipulate these integrated, meaningful wholes. We read a news account of a military adventure and speculate on the chances of all-out war. We listen to a song and compare it to other songs we have heard.

Can computers use rules to manipulate data in these ways? We have seen in Chapter 15 that this is possible. But Dreyfus points out that the programmer must program these manipulative abilities into the computer. He states: "The role of artificial intelligence is to program the computer to do this translating job itself. But it is by no means obvious that the human translator can be disposed of."[9]

In other words, Dreyfus believes that a system is not truly intelligent if it cannot understand spoken language, interpret visual images, and even identify musical pieces. He realizes, of course, that progress has been made in these areas, but he asserts that it has been very limited. And the reason for this is that global rules of translating this type of information have never been found. Instead, researchers have contented themselves with a few very specific rules that will work only in very limited environments; using these rules in a computer would require continual human intervention.

In refuting the psychological assumption, Dreyfus focuses on the basic idea that nervous system operations can be understood in terms of elementary operations. He attacks the idea that humans use the same operations that machines use when tackling similar problems.

For example, the only way that existing computers can estimate depth is through texture gradients. According to this assumption, then, when humans, unaided by machines, make correct estimates of depth, they must consciously or unconsciously make a similar analysis of texture gradients. But Dreyfus points out that assuming that the mind must go through that same process would be similar to assuming that the planets must solve differential equations because they stay in their orbits around the sun. Even an ion solution exhibits a perceptual process in reaching equilibrium. Does this, Dreyfus asks, prove that the ion solution has gone through the same steps that a digital computer would have to go through to make a similar calculation? His point is that, even if all psychological information processing could be done digitally, this does not mean that the mind goes through a similar process. He further asserts that if we are to assume that a subject is using a certain methodology, then the subject must at least sometimes be conscious of using that methodology. Chess masters, for example, may not always be conscious of their methods of problem solving, but if they never report going through a certain process, it would be incorrect to assume they do. This is true even with a chess-playing program, which must go through that process in order to choose the same move.

According to Dreyfus, with some problems—even very simple ones—no set of rules is adequate enough to describe a solving routine. He cites as an example the task of selecting a red square from a collection of shapes of different colors. If a child were given this task, he or she might simply be given three rules: Look at the objects, think about the shape to be chosen, and make a selection. A computer would have to be given much more complex rules. For example, it would have to count the sides of each shape and find one shape with four sides, all of which are equal. But what is a side? The computer might take random points and see if they fall on a line that is the shortest distance between two end points. But how can these points be found? There are no "points" in a jumble of shapes. Humans find points unconsciously, and the counting of the four equal sides may also be done unconsciously. And what about instructions for finding a red square among other squares of different colors. Why, Dreyfus asks, do instructions always end at a certain point? That is, why is there always some point in programming a computer when a human must do some interpreting? Dreyfus claims that it is approximately at this point—when the human interpreter must step in—that the analogy between mind and computer breaks down.

One reason machines have so many problems and need interpreters is that they cannot distinguish between significant and insignificant data, between relevant and irrelevant input. All existing programs require that human programmers explain which data should be used and which should be ignored.

The conclusion to be drawn is that although a person is a physical being who receives input in ways that conform to laws of physics and chemistry, the way that information is processed and stored may have little to do with physics or chemistry. It may be impossible to use a machine to recreate or even simulate human behavior in a real sense.

THE EPISTEMOLOGICAL ASSUMPTION

Even if we grant that human beings do not function according to certain rules, is it not possible to formulate rules that govern human actions? The difference here is between knowing how humans perform a task and formulating rules about human behavior so that a computer can simulate such behavior. That all human behavior can be thus formulated is called by Dreyfus the epistemological assumption.

In a previous example, we spoke of the planets traveling around the sun. They are incapable of solving the differential equations that keep them in their orbits. But it is possible to formulate rules that govern their behavior such that artificial planets can be built to behave in the same way. Another example is a man riding a bike. His ability to keep his balance can be expressed in rules of physics. Obviously, he is not at all aware that he is following these rules. But his behavior can be expressed—and duplicated by a robot—using those rules.

So, if all human behavior can be described by means of such rules, a computer can theoretically be built to simulate human behavior perfectly. The question then is: Can all human behavior be expressed as a set of rules?

Dreyfus provides a number of examples of human behavior that cannot be reduced to sets of rules. One area is language. Can a set of rules be used to make sense of language affected by syntax and semantics? It is certain that a good deal of language can be understood through rules. But although a native speaker may function in a linguistically lawful manner most of the time, he or she will occasionally (or more than occasionally) break a rule. And this breaking of rules is where natural-language researchers often get stuck and where Dreyfus believes he proves that human behavior cannot be formulated.

Take the sentence, "The idea is in the pen." A natural-language process or given knowledge about the size of various objects and about the nature of tangible and intangible objects would be at a loss to decipher this sentence using the rules coded in its program. Yet a native speaker would conclude that, although odd, the sentence does make sense. It probably means that the pen is a tool by which ideas are written down.

So what would most programs do with a sentence like that? A program can treat a sentence in one of two ways. It can see if the sentence follows a set of rules and interpret it according to those rules. This cannot be accomplished with a sentence, so the program must resort to the second method: to relate the sentence as best as the program can to either past sentences or to some knowledge of the world and to take an educated guess. The difference between the machine and the human is that the human has a third alternative: The human can realize that the sentence is odd while still understanding it with a high degree of certainty.

Another problem occurs when a sentence breaks the rules. A human would have little trouble with the phrase, "Snow drive careful," but a computer given rules of usage would be confounded. A limited solution is to include in the computer rules even for poor grammar. But there will always be a situation that defies all the rules. Just one example of this is enough to disprove the intelligence of a machine.

In fact, most natural-language machines are programmed to learn from the user. A salesman using a natural-language front-end system to gain access to a data base is not likely to type "Who bought from I today." So, programming a rule that governs this type of sentence is probably a waste of computer space. But the salesman might type "How'd we do today." When a computer reads a sentence with which it is not familiar, it normally queries the user and then adds to its program new rules based on the knowledge gained from the user. But Dreyfus says that systems such as these, while useful, prove that computers will always fall behind humans and that human-level intelligent behavior in machines is impossible.

THE ONTOLOGICAL ASSUMPTION

This assumption—that facts about the world can be defined, stored, and retrieved in a reasonable way—is, according to Dreyfus, the most fundamental in AI. The first and most basic problem concerns the number of facts that the computer would need. Dreyfus quotes Marvin Minsky[10] as saying that a computer, in order to function with intelligence in the real world, will need approximately 100,000 facts ("one can't find 100 things that he knows 1,000 things about"). Limiting the number of facts in this way doesn't encourage Dreyfus. Even if all knowledge could be expressed by 100,000 facts, how could they be organized and stored so that they could be retrieved in a reasonable amount of time? An acceptable system of classifying knowledge in one field has yet to be discovered. Classifying knowledge of the multitude of fields of human endeavor is a problem without an imaginable solution. And even if such a classification were possible, there would have to be a system that would allow the computer to know when any one particular field should be explored.

Furthermore, understanding something in a specific field usually also requires knowledge of other fields. For example, for a program that reads handwriting, the obvious field of knowledge is that of the physical makeup of letters in all their various forms. But when humans attempt to read illegible handwriting, they bring into play their knowledge of the subject that is written down. Illegible letters or words are deciphered using the context of the sentence.

Another problem is how to deal with the situation that does not consist of a collection of facts, how to deal with recognizing an embarrassing situation, for example, or with determining that something is humorous.

Dreyfus points out that AI programs have been fairly successful in place recognition. In the more vague situation recognition, however, little progress has been made. For example, programs have been developed to recognize the place, home: AT (I, HOME). The place (home) is clear, but the situation is not so clear. I may be in the backyard, but I still consider myself at home. Or I may be in my house, but because I had rented it out, it is no longer my home. How would it be possible to program all the information necessary to explain the renter-rentee relationship? Or how far from home represents "at home"? If a family had been to Europe and then returned to their native country, they might consider themselves "at home" even if they were still a thousand miles from their house. According to Dreyfus, AI researchers concentrate on physical states because in most cases they can be identified and qualified. Situations are too slippery for digital programming.

The problem of understanding ambiguities also shows the need to be able to refer to many different categories of knowledge. For example, in the sentence "He follows Marx," there might be a question as to whether "Marx" refers to Karl or Groucho. The answer lies in the context in which the sentence is set—in the setting, in the tone, in the age of "he," in the political outlook of "he," and so on. The number of possible categories of interpretation in this one simple example is impossibly large. And within each category, the number of facts can be in the hundreds of thousands.

Even if we could develop a program that determines which facts are relevant to a particular situation, the facts themselves might be ambiguous. In the preceding example, "he" could be a communist who followed Groucho for an autograph. The key fact might be that Groucho had been in "his" neighborhood recently. How would the computer determine which fact was more important? Even a computer programmed to store, select, and assign priorities to all the facts based on knowledge both of place and of human intercourse (the situation) would still be uninformed as to the world of nonintercourse (living alone) and nonunique intercourse (tribal living). And then there is the whole range of nonhuman activity.

One proposed solution to the problems in classifying knowledge comes from an understanding of how humans learn. Instead of knowledge being classified by subject, it could be acquired and stored in a continuum of learning. The continuum could be classified according to this step-by-step knowledge building. Our knowledge about each new chair we come across would relate to the last chair we had seen. When the computer sees something it guesses might be a chair, all the knowledge that it learned, chair by chair, would be recalled. But how to program such a hierarchy of concepts? Of course, we could begin with the few concepts that a child is born with and build the structure in a way that is similar to the way a child learns. But leaving aside the need to limit the computer's acquisition of a lot of irrelevant data—which a child automatically forgets—we still have no idea how the infant grows from a set of fixed responses to an ever widening set of variable responses.

Human knowledge, Dreyfus argues, is not programmable. The human ability not only to store hundreds of thousands of bits of information but also to continually classify and reclassify them so that one piece of information might serve to help in many different situations is beyond the scope of a binary computer.

Although Dreyfus sees his work as a refutation of the belief that artificial intelligence is possible, his work also has another value: It lays out many of the inherent limits to AI programming. It is likely that many, if not all, of the problems that Dreyfus points out will never be solved. And in fact, artificial intelligence, by his definition—a machine that can function in all realities as well as a human—may never exist. But whereas Dreyfus's ideas point toward dead ends, toward goals that may never be accomplished, they also provide hints to the detours around those dead ends.

Machines may never be able to hold a reasonable conversation with any human who happens to saunter by. But they may be able to function well in the company of geologists or of people who work in other limited domains. This might not be enough for us to call these machines "intelligent." And perhaps the term "artificial intelligence" promises more than can be delivered. But there is no question that AI systems have improved, and will continue to improve, human life. What may be necessary, though, is a redefinition of goals.

Bibliography

Albus, James Sacra. *Brains, Behavior and Robotics*. Peterborough, NH: Byte Books, 1981.

Barr, Aaron, and Feigenbaum, Edward A. *The Handbook of Artificial Intelligence*. Stanford, CT: Heiristech Press, 1981.

Boden, Margaret A. *Artifical Intelligence and Natural Man*. New York, NY: Basic Books, 1977.

Charniak, Eugene, et al. *Artifical Intelligence Programming*. Hillsdale, NJ: Earlbaum Associates, 1980.

Dreyfus, Hubert. *What Computers Can't Do: A Critique of Artificial Reason*. New York, NY: Harper and Row, 1979.

Ernst, George W., and Newell, Allen. *GPS; A Case Study in Generality*. New York, NY: Academic Press, 1969.

Jaki, Stanley L. *Brains, Mind and Computers*. Frankfurt, West Germany: Herder and Herder, 1969.

Minsky, Marvin Lee, and Papert, Seymour. *Artificial Intelligence*. Eugene, OR: University of Oregon Press, 1973.

Nilsson, Nils J. *Principles of Artificial Intelligence*. Los Altos, CA: Tioga Publishing Co., 1981.

Schank, Roger C., and Riesbeck, Christopher K. *Inside Computer Understanding*. Hillsdale, NJ: Lawrence Erlbaum Associates, 1981.

Slasle, James R. *Artificial Intelligence; The Heuristic Programming Approach*. New York, NY: McGraw-Hill, 1971.

Szotovits, Peter, ed. *Artificial Intelligence in Medicine*. Boulder, CO: Westview Press, 1982.

Winston, Patrick Henry. *Artificial Intelligence*. Boston, MA: Addison-Wesley, 1977.

Winston, Patrick Henry, and Brown, Richard Henry, eds. *Artificial Intelligence; An MIT Perspective*. Cambridge, MA: MIT Press, 1977.

Winston, Patrick Henry. *The Psychology of Computer Vision*. New York, NY: McGraw-Hill, 1978.

Webber, Bonnie Lyne, and Nilsson, Nils J. *Readings in Artificial Intelligence*. Los Altos, CA: Tioga Publishing Co., 1983.

Endnotes

Chapter 2

1. Quoted by Alan Turing in "Computing Machinery and Intelligence," in *Computers and Thought* (Feigenbaum, E.A., ed. New York, NY: McGraw-Hill, 1963).
2. Newell, A., and Simon, H.P. "Empirical Exploration with the Logic Theory Machine," in *Computers and Thought.*
3. Minsky, Marvin. "Descriptive Language and Problem Solving," in *Scientific Information Processing* (Cambridge, MA: MIT Press, 1969).
4. Quoted by Hubert Dreyfus in *What Computers Can't Do: A Critique of Artificial Reason* (New York, NY: Harper and Row, 1979).

Chapter 3

5. Charniak, E. "A Language Comprehension Program," in *Proceedings of the Fifth International Conference on AI—1977* (Pittsburgh, PA: Department of Computer Science, Carnegie Mellon, 1977).

Chapter 5

6. Richards, William. "How to Play Twenty Questions with Nature and Win" (Cambridge, MA: MIT Artificial Intelligence Lab, Dec. 1982).

Chapter 8

7. Corkill, D.D., and Lasser, V.R. "The Distributed Vehicle Monitoring Testbed," in *AI Magazine* (Fall, 1983).

Chapter 9

8. Minsky, Marvin. "Towards a Remotely-Manned Energy and Production Economy" (Cambridge, MA: MIT Artificial Intelligence Lab, Sept. 1979).

Chapter 18

9. Dreyfus, Hubert. *What Computers Can't Do: A Critique of Artificial Reason* (New York, NY: Harper and Row, 1979).
10. *Ibid.*

Index